HOLIDAY CLUB PROGRAMME

for 5- to 11-year olds

© Alex Taylor 2010
First published 2010
ISBN 978 1 84427 511 3

Scripture Union
207–209 Queensway, Bletchley, Milton Keynes, MK2 2EB
Email: info@scriptureunion.org.uk
Website: www.scriptureunion.org.uk

Scripture Union Australia
Locked Bag 2, Central Coast Business Centre, NSW 2252
Website: www.scriptureunion.org.au

Scripture Union USA
PO Box 987, Valley Forge, PA 19482
Website: www.scriptureunion.org

Scripture quotations are from the Contemporary English Version published by HarperCollinsPublishers © 1991, 1992, 1995 American Bible Society.

British Library Cataloguing-in-Publication Data
A catalogue record of this book is available from the British Library.

Printed and bound in Singapore by Tien Wah Press

Cover and internal design: kwgraphicdesign
Cover and internal illustrations: Sean Parkes
Additional material by Alison Dayer, Helen Franklin, Alice Langtree, Steve Hutchinson, Andrew Smith
Additional illustrations: Vicki Barfield, Kevin Wade

✒ Scripture Union is an international charity working with churches in more than 130 countries, providing resources to bring the good news of Jesus Christ to children, young people and families and to encourage them to develop spiritually through the Bible and prayer.

As well as our network of volunteers, staff and associates who run holidays, church-based events and school Christian groups, we produce a wide range of publications and support those who use our resources through training programmes.

For the hundreds of thousands of children who encounter Jesus at a holiday club each year.

CONTENTS

Introduction

MISSION:RESCUE is a seven-day children's holiday club (an opening Sunday service, five club sessions and a closing Sunday service). It has a spies/secret agents theme and explores stories of God rescuing his people, from Exodus 1–15. Children at the club will encounter a God who rescues his people – an amazing, powerful, personal God!

This resource book is packed with creative ideas on how to explore these remarkable stories – ideas you can change and adapt to suit your club and context. There are also ideas for construction (craft), games, drama, creative prayer and worship. MISSION:RESCUE has a mixture of upfront presentation and small group activities, allowing children and leaders to build meaningful relationships with each other and with God.

The holiday club programme is written for the 5 to 11 age group. There are ideas on the MISSION:RESCUE website for extending the age group to include under-5s and/or 11 to 14s. It is for you to decide the best age group for your club, and select the activities to fit.

Every effort has been made to ensure this club programme is suitable for children with little or no church background. It is a tool for churches whose desire is to reach out to children and their families outside their church community. It should work equally well for churches wishing to use it as a discipleship resource for children already part of the church family.

MISSION:RESCUE DVD

This includes five storytelling episodes straight from Secret Agents School! The DVD also contains the MISSION:RESCUE song, backing tracks, training material on using the Bible with children and additional resources.

SECRET FILES

This 48-page booklet contains all the key Bible text taken from the Contemporary English Version, along with small-group material, puzzles and extra information. It is ideal for use with 8 to 11s. Spy Sheets for under-8s are also available in this book (as well as on the DVD and website). There is guidance on how to use both these resources as part of the small group time in each day's programme, and on page 10. Both Secret Files and Spy Sheets help maintain contact with children's homes and act as a reminder, in the weeks after the club, of what the children experienced at MISSION:RESCUE.

More information on these and other resources can be found on the inside front cover. For all details of the publicity materials produced by CPO, see the inside back cover. (Please note, CPO resources are not available through Scripture Union.)

MISSION:RESCUE TERMINOLOGY

AGENTS X AND Y

The presenters of MISSION:RESCUE. They guide children through the session, introducing the different elements and delivering some of the teaching for the day.

SPY CHIEF

The main storyteller, this person retells the story for each day and returns to recap on the main teaching points for the day.

MEMBERS OF THE SECRET SERVICE

The general name for leaders of the club. This is often abbreviated to SSM.

AGENTS

The children at MISSION:RESCUE.

SPY RINGS

The small groups that the children will be part of throughout the club. In these groups, children will explore the Bible, have their refreshments, pray together and maybe do construction and games.

SPYMASTER

Leader of a Spy Ring, helped out by an assistant.

THE CODECRACKERS

The music group for MISSION:RESCUE.

SPY FITNESS INSTRUCTOR

Leads the warm-up and maybe the games too.

HEAD OF SECURITY

Recaps the story of the day so far, and more importantly, the Bible so far, so that the children can remember what has already happened before hearing the next part of the story.

VISIT THE MISSION:RESCUE WEBSITE

Go to www.scriptureunion.org.uk/missionrescue for downloadable versions of the photocopiable pages, Bible discovery notes and material for use with under 5s, 11 to 14s and 14 to 18s young leaders. There's also material for adapting your club to fit three or four days rather than five, information about legal requirements, forms, artwork and logos. You can also read about other people's experiences and check out the advice given by other users on the message boards.

FILE 1

Secret Service mission

The aims of MISSION:RESCUE

MISSION:RESCUE is based around stories about God, Moses and the Israelites from Exodus 1–15, and how God rescued his people from slavery in Egypt. Each day, the children will encounter another episode in the story and explore how God set out to rescue his people in many different ways. Through these stories and themes, the children will also meet Jesus – God's ultimate rescue plan.

MISSION:RESCUE aims to:

- help children discover that God has a plan to save and rescue his people
- invite each and every child to explore what this rescue mission means for them and to encourage them to respond in appropriate ways
- create a fun programme where children will feel welcomed and valued

Theme and setting

MISSION:RESCUE is all about spies or secret agents! As the Agents (the children at the club) explore the Bible stories, they'll have the chance to engage in missions, crack codes, invent secret languages, make disguises and deliver messages. As you set up your venue, think about how you can transform your room into a spy base! This could be as simple as a painted backdrop or two or three TV screens showing secret footage to something as complex as secret equipment hidden behind pieces of set (a little like Mr Smith in The Sarah Jane Adventures!).

The Spy theme is picked up in several different ways:
- The club is introduced and led by two agents, X and Y.
- The children are called Agents and are led by Spymasters.

- Secret clues are used to introduce the Bible stories
- The programme is packed with codes, clues, secret messages and more!

For more ideas and information on setting up your venue, see page 16.

Teaching programme

The story of Exodus is an exciting one, but it's not one without its challenges when using with children. The story has some elements that may seem excessive to our twenty-first century eyes and which require leaders to wrestle with difficult questions. Don't expect children to react in the same way as leaders, though, as children often accept the ways of God much more quickly than adults. Do be ready to help children if they are struggling with aspects of the story. However, the picture of God as one who hears the problems and struggles of his people and reaches down to rescue them is one that all children can identify with in some way. The whole story is packed with rescues, many of which are way outside most children's experience. These will engage the children's interest and help them think about God and what he wants to say to them.

Each day is tightly linked with its theme, so as you embark on each day's mission, you'll be able to focus on what you want the children to learn and take away with them through all the activities. Each day has a concept behind the whole programme, which will be outlined by the presenters at the start of the day. The Bible story is introduced by clues which will help tell the story. These concepts and visual reminders will help the children grasp the main points behind each day's teaching and remember what they have discovered.

Through each day's story and activities, we'll discover more about the character of God, of his love for his people and his desire to save. The character and rescue mission of Jesus is introduced in Mission 4, in connection with the Passover, and developed further in Mission 5. This concept of God rescuing and saving his people in Exodus will allow you to chat about Jesus' mission to rescue and save. If your conversations lead you to talk about Jesus, whatever the day, discussing Jesus and what he means to you should flow naturally.

The Bible teaching is the most important part of the programme, and it should be well planned, prayed through and presented clearly to allow God's Word to settle and grow in the children's minds.

Alongside this is the importance of how you relate to the children, as this reinforces the Bible teaching (as children see you 'practising what you preach'). Jesus said, 'When you welcome even a child because of me, you welcome me. And when you welcome me, you welcome the one who sent me' (Luke 9:48). So as you welcome children, you welcome Jesus; as you talk with them, listen to their stories, laugh at their jokes and cheer their successes. However ordinary these things may be, you are doing them as if to Jesus. Treat the children with the love, respect and dignity with which you would honour him. In addition, children think of Jesus/God in terms of the person who tells them about Jesus/God. You need to 'be' the message as well as giving the message.

MISSION:RESCUE covers seven days: five 'holiday club' days and two Sunday services. If you are running a club which is shorter, go to the MISSION:RESCUE website to check out how to adapt the material for three or four days.

MISSION EXTRA 1 – GOD'S MISSION

Key passage Exodus 1

Key aims
- to see that God's people were in trouble but to discover that God had a rescue plan.
- to kick off MISSION:RESCUE!

Key story We discover the trouble God's people were in, but look forward to God's rescue mission swinging into action!

MISSION 1 – UNDERCOVER

Key passage Exodus 2:1–10 (and 11–25 for 8 to 11s)

Key aims
- to discover that God has a plan to rescue his people.
- to start to understand that God protects us.

- to welcome the children, start building relationships and have fun together.

Key story God rescues Moses, preparing him for the rescue mission.

MISSION 2 – YOUR MISSION, SHOULD YOU CHOOSE TO ACCEPT IT

Key passage Exodus 3:1–15

Key aims
- to realise that God speaks and listens, and will give us everything we need.
- to continue to build relationships with the children, and to welcome those who are new to the club today.

Key story God meets with Moses and gives him the mission to bring his people out of Egypt. He gives Moses everything he'll need to carry out the mission.

MISSION 3 – MISSION ABORT?

Key passage Exodus 5:1–21(retold); 5:22 – 6:13

Key aims
- to find out that God is in control, even when it doesn't look like it.
- to continue to build relationships with the children, and to welcome those who are new to the club today.

Key story Moses starts his mission, but isn't able to persuade Pharaoh to let the Israelites go. Pharaoh makes life worse because of Moses' actions, but God promises that he will rescue his people. The confrontation begins!

MISSION 4 – MISSION ACCOMPLISHED

Key passage (Exodus 7–10 retold) Exodus 11; 12:29–32,33–42

Key aims
- to explore what it means that God rescues and saves, and to respond to God's rescue mission.
- to continue to build relationships with the children, and to introduce Jesus to children with little or no church background.

Key story After the first nine plagues, God's final plague on the Egyptians finally forces Pharaoh to let the people go. God's words are not empty – he does what he says he will do. God's people are saved by sacrificing a lamb and spreading its blood on their doorposts. They share the first Passover together, celebrating God's rescue.

FILE 1

MISSION 5 – ESCAPE!

Key passage   Exodus 14:1–29

Key aims
- to be amazed at how powerful God is and at what he can do, and to respond appropriately.
- to provide a fun final day of the programme for children and to encourage them to return to the Sunday service (if you're having one) and other future events.

Key story   God rescues the Israelites from the chasing Egyptians by miraculously parting the Red Sea. When there was no way out that the Israelites could see, God provided one, using Moses as the instrument for this final rescue of the story. God's people are free!

MISSION EXTRA 2: MISSION DEBRIEF

Key passage   Exodus 15:1–18

Key aims
- to give thanks to God for all he has done, and to look forward to God's plans in the future.
- to celebrate MISSION:RESCUE.

Key story   Moses and the Israelites celebrate their rescue by God and the success of his mission. We too can celebrate! We can thank God for the MISSION:RESCUE club and all we have learned. We can look forward, too, to our continuing relationship with him and our part in his plans.

SAMPLE PROGRAMME

This programme runs for 2 hours 30 minutes, not including preparation and clear-up time (2 hours 15 minutes of planned activities and 15 minutes spare for moving around, overrunning activities ec).

Activity	Running time	Includes
Mission preparation	30 minutes	Spiritual and practical preparation
Agents' briefing Small groups	10 minutes	Introductory activities in Spy Rings
Active agents All together	45 minutes	Upfront Bible teaching, DVD, warm-up, songs, games, Spy Chief, Security report
Going undercover Small groups	45 minutes	Bible discovery, construction, games, refreshments
Agents are go! All together	25 minutes	Teaching recap, interview, songs, drama, Learn and remember verse
Agents' debrief Small groups	10 minutes	Creative prayer, conversation
Mission clear-up	30 minutes	Clearing up, debrief, preparation for next session

Programme breakdown

Each day's programme contains the following elements:

MISSION PREPARATION

Any holiday club's success must be built on prayer. This material provides notes to encourage the team to think and reflect personally on each day's Bible story from Exodus. Before the children arrive, spend some time digging into the Bible story. Pray for each other and pray for the children in your club.

During this time, you'll also need to check that you have everything you need for the session (the equipment checklist for each day is a useful way of doing this), make health and safety checks and ensure everything is ready for the children's arrival.

ARRIVING AT MISSION:RESCUE

The first moments at MISSION:RESCUE are so important! Be welcoming, but not overwhelming, in putting the children and accompanying adults at their ease. Strike a balance between helping parents to see that their children will be safe with you and giving children a sense of the fun that they'll have during the session. Make sure you have enough people at the registration desk (especially on the first day) to show children and their parents to the right groups. It's always helpful to have someone available to answer questions as the parents leave, or to remind them of the collection time, or just say a cheerful, 'See you later!'

REGISTRATION

Make sure that the registration desk is well organised with spare forms and pens for any parents who want to register their children at the door. Have a floor plan of your venue to show where each team is sited, so that parents can find their way round. If possible, have a large plan available a little distance away from the desk so that parents dropping children at more than one group can go back to check the layout without clogging up the registration area.

AGENTS' BRIEFING

This time is not just a fill-in until the last child arrives. During this time the key aims will be relationship-building and feedback. It is a great time to check out who can remember the Learn and remember verse or the story from previous Missions. Each day, there is an introductory activity to do together. These build on the spy theme and allow you plenty of time to chat and build relationships in your Spy Ring. Any Agent with jokes or pictures for the dead letter drop should deliver them as they arrive.

ACTIVE AGENTS

This section of the programme is designed to be fast-moving and fun. The children are all together for Active agents, which is led from the front. It contains the main teaching for the day, together with the other elements outlined below.

X AND Y

Each day, the two main presenters introduce the main theme of the Mission through a spy-related demonstration. This should be quick and fun, engaging the children and making sure they feel welcomed to Active agents. Use this time, too, to go through any health and safety announcements and any rules you have at MISSION:RESCUE.

SPY WORKOUT

This is a fun workout, designed to get the children moving and using up some energy. Use any fast spy-related music and keep the exercises simple. Be aware of any children with special needs and include some actions that they can do. This section works best when it has been well prepared.

SPY SONGS

Children enjoy singing and learning new songs. Choose a mix of songs that some children will know and ones that are new to everyone. The MISSION:RESCUE song is on page 36 and the MISSION:RESCUE DVD. If you have children with little or no church background, avoid confessional songs (songs that express belief or faith), sticking to factual songs ('God is' rather than 'I believe').

SPECIAL OPERATION

This is a team or individual challenge led from the front. Either Spy Rings complete this together or volunteers compete at the front for their Spy Rings. This is a fast-moving section, so if answers need to be given, keep this short and to the point. If the operation is an upfront one, encourage the children to cheer for the volunteers. Each day's operation is different and will need a person from the team to make sure all the resources are ready to use at the right moment.

SECURITY REPORT

This is a recap of what has happened so far in the club and in the story. The Head of Security reminds the children of the story so far and introduces each day's security level (a random choice of colour!).

SPY CHIEF'S CLUES

The Spy Chief is the storyteller of the club and he introduces some clues that he will later use in his storytelling. This is then discussed with X and Y, who might get the input of the children to help decide what the clues mean.

REVEALING THE SECRET

The main storytelling section of the club. The Spy Chief tells the day's story using the clues he brought on earlier. Sometimes this requires the involvement of the children, but each day's storytelling style is slightly different to make sure that this section doesn't become staid.

The MISSION:RESCUE DVD contains five storytelling episodes, helping you tell the Bible story. If you don't have any strong storytellers, you may choose the DVD as the primary storytelling tool. Alternatively, you might choose to do the live retelling and reinforce it with the DVD. See page 4 for more details about the DVD.

CHECKING THE EVIDENCE

This is a short quiz to recap the facts of the story, and some of the events of the Mission so far. Some suggestions for questions are given for each Mission, but you'll need to add more of your own questions. To score the quiz, create a secret spy scoring machine. This can be easily created with a vacuum cleaner and some ping-pong balls! Write a different number on each of the ping-pong balls and put them in a bucket or large bowl. Use the hose attachment of a vacuum cleaner to suck up one of the balls, and the Spy Ring is awarded the number of points written on that ball. You can disguise the vacuum cleaner, turning it into a complicated and state-of-the-art spy gadget! (This was first used on the SU holiday Ka'zoo. See MISSION: RESCUE website for pictures.)

TODAY'S MISSION

Agents X and Y review the teaching points of the story. Make this punchy and to the point, so that it doesn't go over the children's heads – it should leave the children thinking and challenged!

THE GODCODE

This is a time of praying all together which uses a prayer action or shout; one that when the children see/hear it, they know they're going to be talking to God. This is short and to the point.

GOING UNDERCOVER

The Agents move into their Spy Rings for refreshments, Bible exploration, construction and games. You can choose to do the construction and games in Spy Rings or all together. It depends on what team and facilities you have.

THE MAD LABORATORY

This is the time when the Agents have their refreshments. You could make some cookies with secret messages inside, perhaps Bible verses to decode. (Do a search on the Internet for fortune cookies to find out how to do this.) Or create the feeling of a mad laboratory, with lab technicians coming up with crazy food to eat. You could make exploding snacks (for example, a simple biscuit recipe, topped with popping candy) and different drinks. Use your imagination to come up with refreshments that fit this mad inventing theme. Decorate the space with test tubes and other lab equipment filled with coloured liquids.

BIBLE DISCOVERY

This time allows the children to develop skills in thinking about the meaning of the Bible and how it applies to their life. The Bible exploration can be done using Secret Files (for 8 to 11s) or Spy Sheets (for 5 to 8s), through discussions or a combination of both. Photocopiable notes for Spymasters are available on the MISSION:RESCUE website. Make sure all Spymasters and assistants are prepared for this vital time. For more information about leading a small group, see Top Tips on Leading small groups.

Q-TECH'S WORKSHOP AND SPIES' TIME OUT

Construction/craft and games used during MISSION: RESCUE can be found on pages 27-32. For further inspiration, see Ultimate Craft and Ultimate Games, which each contain hundreds of ideas that might be suitable for your club. Make sure you risk-assess these activities and collect all the necessary materials beforehand. These times are another good opportunity for leaders and children to chat and build relationships.

AGENTS ARE GO!

During this time, the children are all together for activities led from the front.

DEAD LETTER DROP

As the children return from their Spy Rings, X and Y should read some of the messages and jokes left in the dead letter drop. On Mission 1, X and Y should explain that a dead letter drop is where Agents can secretly leave their jokes and messages and that, each day, they will read out some of the jokes and show some of their pictures.

RETURN OF THE SPY CHIEF

Here, the Spy Chief returns and recaps the teaching points from the story and what the children have discovered during Going undercover. Again this should be punchy and to the point. This is not a talk, but a recap.

INTERROGATION

Each day, a different member of the Secret Service is interviewed (or interrogated!). Choose the SSM carefully, as they need to have a story that relates to the day's theme and is suitable to be shared with the children. This interview gives the children the chance to see how the Bible teaching relates to everyday life. Each day, encourage the children to write down any questions they'd like to ask the SSM. These can be related to the theme, or about their general life and likes – favourite colour, pet etc!

DRAMA: WHO'S THE MOLE?

The secret papers for Operation Moses Rescue have been stolen and agents M, O, S, E and Z are sent on a mission to catch the perpetrators and retrieve the papers. But a message comes in by carrier pigeon (along with another deposit!) that warns them of a mole in their midst. The drama is not designed to be a primary teaching tool, but a reinforcement of the theme and a chance for some slapstick fun!

CRACKING THE CODE

Each day, the children will be challenged to learn the verse for the week (Psalm 118:24). A different activity is given each day to help learn the verse, and the Learn and remember verse song is also available (see the MISSION:RESCUE website and the MISSION:RESCUE DVD). The Learn and remember verse is the same for the whole week, but you could come up with a different verse for each day. The different activities will work with any verse.

COMPLETING THE MISSION

This wraps up the all together time with the theme song and maybe another song the children have enjoyed. Include a prayer here too, thanking God for your time together.

AGENTS' DEBRIEF

The Mission draws to a close in small groups. Each day there is a creative prayer activity for the Spy Rings to do. Alternatively, you could finish off anything from the club that still needs work (pages from Secret Files or the construction).

Spymasters should make a point of saying goodbye to each child and reminding them of the next session.

MISSION CLEAR-UP

It may be that some of the team have their own children at MISSION:RESCUE and are unable to stay for long when the programme ends. As a minimum, have everyone together to check any problems, briefly remind people of tomorrow's activities and pray for the Holy Spirit to be at work in the children.

If you have time and the facilities, the team could share lunch together to round off the Mission.

Other elements of MISSION:RESCUE

SERVICES

The programme contains two services, one to start the club and one to finish. Whereas in previous SU programmes, the first service has been more of an information-giving and commissioning service for the congregation and team, MISSION:RESCUE's first service is designed to be an integral part of the club for children. This is to help you encourage children from outside your church community and their families to come into a church service. Research shows that if you advertise the club as including the services as well as the club days (so a seven-day programme rather than a five-day one), children and families with little or no church background are more likely to attend. However, children who don't attend this first service will still find it easy to join the club on Day 1. It is a great idea to commission the team and get your congregation praying, and you should think about doing this the service before the first Sunday of MISSION:RESCUE. This means that the first Sunday service of the club has a clear aim (and an earlier commissioning will encourage the church to pray as you prepare, as well as when the club is taking place).

UNDER-5s RESOURCES

For details of resources to use with 5s and under, visit the MISSION:RESCUE website. The resources follow the same Bible passages and themes as the main programme.

11 TO 14s RESOURCES

For details of resources to use with 11 to 14s, visit the MISSION:RESCUE website. The resources follow the same Bible passages and themes as the main programme.

14 TO 18s – YOUNG LEADERS

Having young people help out at a holiday club is a fantastic way of discipling and training them in leadership. For training materials for use specifically with 14 to 18s in leadership, go to the MISSION: RESCUE website.

FAMILY ACTIVITIES

It is a good idea to include some events in your club for families to attend all together. This will give you a chance to meet and get to know the families of children who are coming to MISSION:RESCUE. Get your whole church involved in organising food or running activities. Here are a few things you could try:

- **Secret agent games**: organise a family games event, using some of the games ideas from pages 30-32. Families could work together, or you could pair a family from your church community with one new to the church, to help build relationships.

- **Operation**: construction: similarly to the games event, use some of the construction ideas on pages 27-30 to put together a family session. Activities such as woodturning, pyrography and other more robust crafts are great for encouraging family members to work together (for instance, fathers and sons). You could combine construction and games into one event.
- **Passover**: include some of the elements of the Passover meal into an event for families. This would work particularly well if it were run on the same day as you did Mission 4 in your club. For more information and guidance on running an event of this kind, go to the MISSION:RESCUE website.
- **Family barbecue**: these events are always popular and can be quite simple to run! Alongside the food, you could run games or construction. Or how about a family quiz? Ask questions about spy films or the story of Moses (for the children).

None of these ideas are groundbreaking in themselves but, run in conjunction with the club, they can involve more of the church community in the club, introduce the church to people with little or no previous contact in a relaxed atmosphere and start to build relationships.

FILE 2

Mission details

Planning MISSION: RESCUE

When starting to think about running a holiday club, some big issues need to be tackled:

DEFINE YOUR AIMS

The broad aims of MISSION:RESCUE are on page 6, but each individual holiday club will have its own specific aims. MISSION:RESCUE can provide a manageable, creative and fun way of reaching out to the children of your neighbourhood with the good news of Jesus. It can provide an excellent opportunity to blow any misconceptions away and to reveal to them a God who loves them passionately.

Here are some aims which you might choose for your club:
- To attract new children to join your Sunday groups or other children's activities.
- To develop your leaders' gifts and experience.
- To present the gospel to children who've never heard it.
- To provide an opportunity for children to make an initial or further commitment to follow Jesus.
- To get to know the children in your church.
- To provide a project to encourage your church to work together.
- To establish links with the children's families.
- To encourage cooperation with other churches or groups in your area.
- To launch an ongoing children's group based on the MISSION:RESCUE theme.
- To give parents a few mornings off in the school holidays.

Any or all of these aims may be appropriate, but you'll have to decide what you want MISSION:RESCUE to achieve in your situation. If you have several aims,

you'll need to decide which are the most important. You'll also need to evaluate MISSION:RESCUE afterwards, to see if you met your aims. Decide now how you'll do that. How will you measure success? Try the aims form on the MISSION:RESCUE website or DVD to focus your aims and help the rest of your team buy into the aims you have set.

THE CHILDREN

Once you have set your aims, you'll be able to make other key decisions such as:

WHO WILL YOU INVITE TO MISSION:RESCUE?

Do your aims relate to the children already involved in your church, or those outside it?

How many children do you want to involve? If your main aim is to get to know the children better, you might need to restrict numbers. On the other hand, if you want to present the gospel to children who haven't heard it, you may want as many as possible to attend.

What age range(s) do you want to target with MISSION: RESCUE? Do you want to cater for an age range that is well represented in your groups, or one that isn't? Will you be able to tailor the activities in a way that will appeal to a wide age range? MISSION:RESCUE is designed for use with children between the ages of 5 and 11 but the MISSION:RESCUE website also has a programme for use with under-5s and one for use with 11 to 14s.

WHEN WILL YOU RUN YOUR CLUB, AND FOR HOW LONG?

You'll need to fix the date for your holiday club early enough for people to take it into account when they book their holidays. It is also essential that the dates do not clash with other holiday clubs in the area, activities already booked at your premises, holidays organised by local schools, holidays/camps for local Boys' Brigade, Girls' Brigade, Cub or Brownie groups, and carnivals or local events taking place in your area.

The potential leaders' availability will have the most effect on the duration of your holiday club. If most of your leaders need to take time off work, it may not be practical to run a full five-day club.

If you are planning to run your club over three or four days, rather than five, go to the MISSION:RESCUE website (www.scriptureunion.org.uk/missionrescue) for guidance on how to adapt the material for a shorter club.

LEGAL REQUIREMENTS

There are various legal requirements you will need to be familiar with and conform to as you prepare for your holiday club. These include having a child protection policy in place, providing adequate space in your venue, meeting adult to child ratios, insurance. To obtain up-to-date information on all of these requirements, go to the downloads section of the MISSION:RESCUE website under 'Legal requirements for running a club'.

FINANCES

You'll need to consider your financial resources. Work out what you'll need money for. Examples might include:

- craft materials
- refreshments
- materials for the scenery
- photocopying/printing costs
- hire of premises
- hire of equipment such as a video projector
- MISSION:RESCUE resource books for your leaders
- resources such as the MISSION:RESCUE DVD and Secret Files
- prizes or presents for the children

Do you need to do some fund-raising? Or will you charge a small fee for children to attend MISSION:RESCUE? Research shows that in many cases, making a charge for a club has no effect on the number of children who come. Indeed, some parents may value a club they have had to pay for more highly than something that is free.

PUBLICITY

The best way to ensure you have plenty of children at your holiday club is for the event to be well publicised.

There is material available from CPO to help you with this. See the inside back cover for details. Here are some things to consider:

POSTERS AND FLYERS

Use these to advertise MISSION:RESCUE.

LETTERS AND FORMS

How about sending a letter or invitation card to every child your church has contact with? Or you might distribute letters to all the children in your area, maybe through the local schools. Your letter could enclose an application/registration form to be returned to you. You may also need a follow-up letter, which will enclose a consent/medical form, and perhaps a MISSION:RESCUE identity badge.

SCHOOL ASSEMBLIES

You may have a local Christian schools worker, or people from your church who are involved in schools ministry. Or you may have some church members who are teachers. If so, they could promote your MISSION:RESCUE event in a school assembly, if the school is happy for them to do so.

PRESS RELEASES

Holiday clubs provide the kind of story that local papers love to cover. By getting a story in the press, you'll increase the appeal of your holiday club and show that the church(es) involved are reaching out into your local community. By mentioning Scripture Union's name it increases our awareness, which ultimately allows us to improve resources like our holiday club material. If you have a good relationship with your local press, then make contact in the usual way and inform them of your event. If this is something you have never considered, a press release template is available on the MISSION:RESCUE website. Include your club's details and send the press release to your local paper.

PRAYER CARDS/BOOKMARKS

It is important to keep your church informed about your event. Prayer cards or prayer bookmarks can help your church members pray for your holiday club – before, during and after your MISSION:RESCUE event.

PLAN IN DETAIL

In the few months before MISSION:RESCUE, you'll need to consider and organise the following aspects.

PRESENTATION AND TEACHING

How will you adapt the material to suit your particular age group(s)? What audio/visual aids will you need? Will you need amplification or video projection equipment? Who will be Agents X and Y?

PROGRAMME PRIORITIES

You may not have time to fit in all the activities that are suggested. Within Spy Rings times, especially during Going undercover, you could get so engrossed in general conversation that you never start on the Bible discussions, so be sure to plan carefully.

Imagine filling a jar up to the top with pebbles. You might think it is now full, but try adding some smaller stones and you'll find there is room for them. Is it full now? Try pouring in water, and you will see that only then is the jar really full. But if you put in this amount of either small stones or water first you would not then get everything in! When planning, make sure you put in the essentials first – upfront Bible teaching and discussion time in groups. Then add the less vital but still important things, and finally the parts that 'fill it up'.

MUSIC

Choose the songs for the week, and gather the musicians together to rehearse them. It's good to have a number of musicians playing a variety of instruments, but you'll need to make sure you have enough stage space for other things too! Choose a few new songs and a few old favourites. Make sure you include non-confessional songs, so that the children are not singing words they might not believe. If you don't have musicians in your team, you could use backing tracks or simply sing along to a CD/MP3.

DRAMA

Do you need to adapt the script to fit the number or gender of your cast members, or the limitations of your venue? How much rehearsal time will you need? How will you obtain or make the necessary props, costumes and scenery?

TRAINING

Undertaking some basic skills and knowledge training is vital for the success of the holiday club. You should aim to have at least two sessions together in preparation, and you should ensure that these are more or less compulsory for team members. As part of these sessions, the vision and practicalities of MISSION:RESCUE can also be outlined. Training is outlined in Part 3.

GOING UNDERCOVER

You'll need to think about how you are going to stage this small-groups/craft/games time. What you do depends on your aims and the resources you have available.

- You could have every Spy Ring doing the same activity on the same day. This means that only one simple explanation from the front is needed, and group leaders can help each other. It also helps to develop relationships within the Spy Ring. This does, however, require a lot of resources, and activities which suit this format are limited.
- Alternatively, you could set up activities for the whole week and children rotate around these activities. This means fewer resources are needed for each activity, more activities are possible, and different leaders can take responsibility for leading the same activity each day. However, it is harder to theme each activity to the day's teaching. Some groups will not have their Spymaster with them during this time if they are leading another activity. You will probably also need specific areas that can be dedicated to each activity, and your venue may not be large enough.

CONSTRUCTION/CRAFT

Where will you get the necessary materials and equipment? Do you need to ask your congregation to collect particular items? A dedicated craft team can be very useful, especially in the run-up to MISSION: RESCUE. This team should collect the necessary materials etc. They'll also be able to make templates and patterns for the children to draw around or cut out. The craft team should make up prototypes of the craft, and pass on any hints to the Spymasters.

Involve local schools in amassing reusable material to use during the week (glass jars, plastic bottles, travel magazines for collage etc). This gets people actively contributing to the club before it has begun, including the children!

GAMES

Consider what games you can play based on the number of children, your venue and the equipment you have. Make sure you have all the equipment you need.

DATA PROTECTION

How will you maintain the confidentiality of the information you receive on the registration forms? Make sure your church is registered under the Data Protection Act. Visit www.informationcommissioner. gov.uk and click on 'Data protection'.

ACCIDENTS

Make sure you have at least one person appointed as a first-aider with a current first aid certificate and access to an up-to-date first aid kit. The whole team should know who is responsible for first aid. You will also need an accident book to record any incidents. This is essential in the event of an insurance claim. The matter should be recorded, however small, along with details of the action taken. Visit www.rospa.co.uk for other health and safety information.

FIRE PROCEDURES

It is essential that the whole team knows emergency procedures, including fire exits and assembly points, and where to access a telephone in case of emergency. Ensure you keep all fire exits clear.

PRAYER TEAM

Make sure you have a team of people committed to pray throughout the preparation and the club itself. Keep the whole church well-informed too. The prayer team should keep on praying for the children in the club in the months after MISSION:RESCUE finishes.

USE OF THE BIBLE

One of the aims of MISSION:RESCUE is to help children explore and read the Bible for themselves. So each day during Going undercover, when you move on to discussing the passage, help them find it in the Bible or Secret Files and learn to look for answers there. Use a translation that is easy for children to read (Good News Bible, Contemporary English Version or International Children's Bible).

SET THE SCENE

Choosing a venue is a very important issue. Sometimes a community hall or school is a well-equipped, neutral venue that can be non-threatening for children and parents outside the church. However, you may wish to use this opportunity to introduce the children and parents to your church building. This can also help save on the cost of hiring an alternative venue. The venue does need to have enough space for the number of children and the type of activities you are planning. You will need access to the venue before the holiday club to ensure the necessary preparations can be made.

SETTING UP THE ROOM

The holiday club will be greatly enhanced if the main room you are using is transformed into a spy-centre! This will help create a wonderful atmosphere and spark the children's imagination. You will need to think creatively about how you can transform your venue into an exciting place. The imaginative use of cardboard, wood, paint and other materials can make a real difference. Think about what you can hang from the ceiling, cover the walls with and put on the floor. It may be that someone in your area has already done MISSION: RESCUE and has scenery and decorations you could borrow. Go to www.scriptureunion.org.uk/missionrescue and click on 'Bulletin board'.

To transform your area, you could:

- Set up the stage with TV screens, computers and other high-tech equipment, so that the stage area looks like a busy and active spy-centre. Have various different DVDs and visuals on the screens, from news programmes, programmes such as MI High or The Secret Show or the MISSION:RESCUE logo.
- If you are particularly adventurous, you could have spy equipment hidden behind furniture, fireplaces or paintings – think Mr Smith from The Sarah Jane Adventures.
- Encourage the team to wear spy outfits (all black, or a fedora/homburg), or come in ridiculous disguises!

SPY RING LOCATIONS

The rest of the room can be split up into Spy Ring locations. You could colour-code the locations to help the children know where their group meets or use some other kind of visual code. It may be best to keep chairs out of the way, except for those who cannot sit on the floor, so that the room can be used for the energetic sections of the programme without objects getting in the way.

FILL THE SCREEN

If you are using a video projector or OHP, use a default image when it is not being used, so that the screen is never blank. Use something simple, like the MISSION: RESCUE logo or some photos of high-tech equipment or action shots of people doing risky pursuits. The logo and other artwork are available on the DVD-ROM section of the MISSION:RESCUE DVD or on the website.

FILE 3

Secret Service training

DEVELOPING PEOPLE'S POTENTIAL

As well as being a time of great fun and development for the children attending, a holiday club is also an important time for the adults leading and helping out. Helping with a holiday club can be a big step for people in the development of their gifts and ministry.

How does a holiday club develop people's potential?
- It involves people in the church who don't usually work with children.
- It is an opportunity for people of all ages to work together in a way that may not happen at any other time of the year. (A regular comment at one holiday club from team members is, 'This is the best week of the year in church!' It's probably the most demanding and tiring too!)
- It develops people's gifts and lets them take risks.
- It discovers people's untapped gifts and enthusiasms.
- It provides a structure for the overall leadership of the club/church to seek out and encourage people to 'have a go'. (The age of volunteering has passed so don't rely on issuing a general plea for volunteers. Look at who you have available and ask people personally, giving them good reasons why you think they could fulfil whatever task you have identified. That suggests that you believe in them! They are far more likely to agree to get involved!)

AREAS OF RESPONSIBILITY

A successful holiday club team requires a variety of support teams to be set up and individuals taking responsibility for different areas of the programme. Listed below are some of the different teams you will need and some of the key roles people will need to assume before, during and after the event. Some people will be able to play more than one role for MISSION: RESCUE.

CORE PLANNING TEAM

All the members of the Secret Service should be involved in the planning and preparing for MISSION: RESCUE, but you will need a smaller team to coordinate things and make some initial decisions. As well as the holiday club's overall leader, this should include your most experienced leaders, your minister and your children's workers.

AGENT M

This is the overall leader, ideally someone who is not involved in the presentation. Their role would be to:
- Make any on-the-spot decisions such as accepting extra children at the door.
- Keep the whole programme to time, moving things on when necessary.
- Look at quality of presentation, watching out for problems such as too much banter between team and Agents X and Y.
- Watch out for children who are not joining in well and help them to become part of things.
- Being the person to whom everyone would report in the event of a fire.

AGENTS X AND Y

These are the upfront presenters of the club. They should be confident on stage and have experience of leading a programme in a fun and flexible manner. These two people will be called upon to do some acting/improvising at the start of each club, so they should be confident enough to do that. In the programme, X is the smarter of the two. X is written as a woman and Y as a man, but the gender of the two presenters is not important.

SPY CHIEF

This person is the storyteller. As such, they must be a confident and skilled communicator. They need to prepare the story thoroughly and be happy telling it to a group of children. You could use a different person each day, if you don't have one member of the team who could put in this much work. You could even make a joke that X and Y think the Chief is one person in a different disguise every day!

SPYMASTERS

Each small group needs a leader. This Spymaster should be at the club every day and will be the person with whom the children have the most personal contact. The leader's role is to get to know the children so that they feel welcome and comfortable at MISSION: RESCUE. The programme is designed to give the Spymaster enough time in their Spy Rings to have meaningful discussions, including ones that apply the teaching programme to the children's lives.

They should coordinate all small-group activities and sit with their Spy Ring during the upfront times. The Spymaster should have a copy of the register, be aware of any special needs and ensure that children all leave safely at the end of the day's session.

ASSISTANTS

The role of the Assistant is to support the Spymaster and ideally should also be available every day. This is a good way to develop the leadership skill of young or inexperienced team members.

All team members should be given training in dealing with children, especially in relation to physical contact and not being with children alone out of sight of others, but Spy Masters and Assistants especially need to be aware of child protection issues and policies.

If you have a large holiday club, you may choose to appoint Spy Ring coordinators to oversee six or eight Spy Rings who are all in one age range. It is best if these coordinators do not have a group of their own.

HEAD OF SECURITY

Gives the 'security report', which outlines what has happened in the story so far. This would be a good way to give less-experienced team members a chance to develop presentation skills.

SPY FITNESS INSTRUCTOR

Leads the aerobic activity each day (and could lead the games too). They should be dressed in a tracksuit. They should put together a set of simple exercises that the children can do (bearing in mind any children with special needs that you might have in the club).

THE CODECRACKERS

Having a live band can add something special to a holiday club. If you can't have live music, you could sing along to a CD.

DRAMA TEAM

A small team of three people should take responsibility for the MISSION:RESCUE drama. These people need to be reasonably confident as actors with the ability to project their voice. The prewritten sketches are somewhat messy and silly and will need some coordination. The team should be willing to learn their lines and to practise each sketch until they can perform it with confidence.

One of the drama team (or another person) needs to take the responsibility of Props Manager, and collect and prepare all the props.

PRINTING AND PUBLICITY TEAM

A small team, including at least one computer-literate person, should take responsibility for all the design, printing and publicity for MISSION:RESCUE. Your aim should be to produce publicity that is visually impressive, consistent, accurate and attractive.

The publicity will need to be colourful, and use the MISSION:RESCUE logo (available on the DVD or website), an attractive, child-friendly font, pictures and clip art. The publicity team should take responsibility for:

- Posters and fliers to advertise MISSION:RESCUE.
- Registration forms for the children to fill in (see sample version on the website).
- Consent forms for parents/guardians/carers (see sample version on the website).
- Invitation cards or letters to go with the appropriate forms.
- Forms for potential team members, including an indication of roles they'd like to take on. You should also send CRB/ISA forms out with these forms if the team member has not already had clearance.
- Notes and training materials for the team. Even if someone else writes this material, the printing and publicity team should be responsible for the layout.
- Name badges for the team members and for any adults who are on site and part of MISSION:RESCUE.
- Signs and notices. These will be needed around the site, including the main hall, entrances, toilets and areas that are out of bounds. These should use the same typeface and colours as other materials to maintain the consistent MISSION:RESCUE scheme.

- Prayer cards/bookmarks – prayer pointers to help church members to pray for the holiday club before, during and after MISSION:RESCUE events.

CPO produce a wide range of MISSION:RESCUE publicity or other merchandise. For details, see the inside back cover.

REGISTRATION TEAM

Responsible for:
- Allocation of children to groups.
- Checking children in and out each day.
- Checking forms are completed fully.
- Keeping a check on team sizes if more children register during MISSION:RESCUE.
- Ensuring each child is to be picked up or has permission to walk home by themselves. If you have a lot of children attending the club, it can be hard to keep track of who has permission to collect which child, especially when parents help each other out. A collection slip, which can be given to the adult who will pick the child up, is on the MISSION:RESCUE website.

If you are advertising the club through a local school or community groups, provide children with booking forms in advance which can be filled out and sent back to the leader of the holiday club, school office or community group leader. This allows you to allocate children to groups in advance and will inform you of dietary requirements, medical issues and physical, educational or behavioural special needs. A register can be made, based on the names and ages provided. A copy of a register must also be given to each group leader in case of a fire or emergency.

In some contexts, pre-registering is not practical, therefore ensure on the first day that there are plenty of volunteers available to help greet the children and their parents or carers and to provide them with the registration form to fill in. Children should not attend the event if permission has not been granted. As this can be a lengthy process, you might like to open the doors earlier on Day 1 and during registration engage the children in parachute games, upfront games or a short film.

REFRESHMENT TEAM

This team will play a vital role during the week. They will be responsible for:
- Checking with the registration team that you have no children with food allergies.
- Obtaining and preparing the refreshments for the children.
- Tidying up after the refreshments have been given out.

For this team to work efficiently you may like to choose one person to coordinate the group. If you are providing anything more than a drink and a biscuit, you should have someone with a food hygiene certificate. Think about using (recyclable) disposable cups or bottles to save on washing-up time.

SECURITY

The person in charge of security will be responsible for ensuring that no child leaves the building unless they have permission to do so, and that only children or adults who are part of MISSION:RESCUE are allowed to enter the building.

It is important for each adult to have an appropriate, clearly labelled badge to identify them and their role. The children registered for MISSION:RESCUE should have their own badge. Any adult or child on site not wearing an appropriate badge should be challenged.

FIRST-AIDER

Aim to have at least one member of your team with a valid first aid certificate. If possible have assistants too – a male for the boys and a female for the girls. These people will need a current first aid certificate, and access to a first aid kit. You will also need an accident book to record any incidents or accidents. (This is essential in the event of any insurance claim. A record of the matter should be noted, along with details of action taken. It should be countersigned where appropriate.)

HEALTH AND SAFETY PERSON

This person will need to plan how you will evacuate the building in the event of a fire. Check that fire escapes are kept clear, that the team know the position of fire extinguishers, and know what the fire alarm – or noise that means 'leave the building immediately' – sounds like. Each Spymaster should be a roll-call marshal for their teams. The health and safety person is in charge of clearing the building and dealing with the emergency services, but they should allocate responsibility for checking other areas of the building (toilets, snack bar etc) to other team members who will be present each day. You may want to incorporate a fire drill into your programme early in the week. The children will be used to this from school, but it might help the adults!

They should also make sure all the activities are adequately risk-assessed before the club starts.

CONSTRUCTION AND EQUIPMENT

Someone should take responsibility for making sure

that everything that is needed for the construction (craft), creative prayer and Spy Ring activities is in the correct place at the right time. Get as much as possible of the craft prepared in advance; there may well be church members who, while they can't help at the club itself, will be happy to help with cutting out etc.

Try to prepare a finished version of each item to show the children what they are making, and providing everything needed for each team's vanity case (pens, paper, modelling clay etc). Each day, one of the craft team should explain how the construction is made and supervise the activity, even if it is done in Spy Rings.

TECHNICAL MANAGER

The amount of technology used will vary with the size and nature of each club. A technical manager could take responsibility for:

- Visual – OHP or laptop and projector, screen, or DVD and TV.
- Audio – PA for presenters and band, CD/MP3 player.

Training your team

However experienced your team, there are two key areas to cover in training: good practice in working with children and delivering the MISSION:RESCUE programme itself. Here is a suggested programme for two training sessions. However, this material could easily be spread over several sessions.

SESSION 1

- **Practicalities**: Basic outline of MISSION:RESCUE, learning the theme song, daily structure etc.
- **Skills**: Leading a small group (incorporating dealing with challenging behaviour)
- **Skills**: Praying with children
- **Skills**: Reading the Bible with children
- **Prayer**: For MISSION:RESCUE and all who come

SESSION 2

- **Meaning**: The cross where Jesus died: God's ultimate MISSION:RESCUE
- **Skills**: Helping children respond to Jesus
- **Understanding**: Working with special or additional needs
- **Understanding**: Working with children from other faith backgrounds
- **Prayer**: For MISSION:RESCUE and all who come

SESSION 3

- **Skills**: Using the Bible with children
  - Why it matters
  - How to do it
  - With early or reluctant readers
- **Skills**: Sharing Bible stories; communicating God in non-book ways; exploring the Bible with Children
- **Practicalities**: Getting the best from the DVD training feature

SESSION 1
THE MISSION:RESCUE PROGRAMME AND CHILDREN

Use this session to go through some of the practical aspects of the club, to help your team understand what will be expected of them and to begin to consider the children who will come to MISSION:RESCUE.

WELCOME

Make sure you give the team a big welcome, ensuring refreshments are freely available, with the MISSION: RESCUE theme song playing in the background as people arrive.

PRACTICALITIES
MISSION:RESCUE

Explain the overall themes of MISSION:RESCUE (see page 6) and explain a little of God's plan to save and rescue his people. Give an overview of the different roles that people will have. Introduce the team to the Learn and remember verse (Psalm 118:24), the MISSION:RESCUE theme song, the Spy Chief, Agents X and Y and the other recurring elements of the programme.

Take the team through a day's programme, making sure that everyone knows where all the different parts will take place and their responsibilities in each one.

The aims of MISSION:RESCUE

Make sure everyone has a copy of the general aims of MISSION:RESCUE (see page 6) and the specific aims for your club. Split into smaller groups to discuss these aims – can the groups identify any other aims? This will help you refine your aims and encourage your team to take ownership of them.

Practicalities

Cover health and safety, risk assessments, fire procedures and basic child protection (go to www.scriptureunion.org.uk/holidayclubs for more information). If your church has a coordinator for this, they should be able to help out at this point. Alternatively, contact CCPAS or visit their website: www.ccpas.co.uk

LEADING A SMALL GROUP

Leading a small group of children is a vital part of MISSION:RESCUE. Spymasters will be the ones who get to know and build relationships with the children, in their small group Spy Rings. Sometimes these relationships can develop into long-term friendships. Understanding how these groups work and having a set of guidelines are really important.

SMALL-GROUP ROLE PLAY

If you have a fairly confident group of leaders, try this role play activity. Six or seven leaders play typical children in a group, and one leader is the Spymaster. This small group is going to look at the Spy Sheets activity from Day 1 (see page 58). Split your team into groups of seven or eight, and make sure you provide enough sets of the character descriptions (see below) and everything that you need for the Spy Sheets activity.

Give out the character descriptions and tell the teams not to show anyone their piece of paper, but to act it out during the activity as best they can. Encourage the team not to overact and make their group leader's role a total nightmare, but to take it as seriously as they can.

- You are the Spymaster. Your group has lots of needs, and you should try very hard to include everyone in the discussion and keep the discussion on track!
- You are an intelligent child who knows all the answers and keeps putting their hand up to answer, or to ask a question, but you don't call out or interrupt.
- You are a very shy younger child, who will be very slow in interacting with the group.
- You are a fidgeter who can't keep still, yet is following what is being discussed.
- You are a child who naturally interrupts all the time, but should respond to firm handling by your Spymaster. You should ask to go to the toilet at least once during the short group time.
- You are an average sort of child, who is interested in the teaching and discussion. You have got a bit of a crush on your leader, so go and sit next to them if you can and maintain eye contact.
- You listen well and follow all that your leader asks you to do, making a valuable contribution to the group.
- You are deeply committed to Jesus and yet find it very difficult to articulate how you feel or what to say. You try very hard to contribute to the group.

Feedback from the role play

The activity should be a good, fun way of raising some of the issues involved in leading a small group. Have some flip chart paper and markers ready to note down any interesting points to come from the groups.

Talk first to the Spymasters, encouraging them that at MISSION:RESCUE it will never be as difficult as the last few minutes! Ask them to outline the characters in their group. What was difficult to deal with? Who contributed? Who didn't contribute and why?

Discuss some of the issues raised by the characters, eg how are you going to handle children going to the toilet? How should you handle leader crushes?

By the time the feedback has finished you should have a set of guidelines for leading a group. Below are a few dos and don'ts which may be worth adding to discussion at the end.

Dos and don'ts of leading a small group

- Do learn their names and call them by name.
- Do take notice of how each child behaves, reacts and interacts so you can get to know each one quickly.
- Do take the initiative. Let them know clearly what you expect from the group, how each one is valued and encouraged to participate in the life of the group.
- Do be specific in your prompting and questions (this can help everyone contribute).
- Do try to meet the children's needs (each child will come with their own needs).
- Don't assume that all the children will learn from or experience the club in the same way.
- Do be polite and patient (even if one or two children really annoy you!).
- Do add oodles of enthusiasm to your group (they will pick up on your attitude – you are a role model).
- Do think creatively eg how you sit, lie or kneel as a group to discuss things. One way would be for everyone in the group (including leaders) to lie on the floor on their tummies in a circle with heads in to the centre – highly appropriate for spies who do not want to be overheard, but it is also much easier to hear one another.
- Do model what you expect the children to do, eg response to the stage.
- Do be careful to follow closely any instructions or notes you are given.
- Do ask for help if you need it (you are not alone!).
- Do be careful with language (no jargon, complicated or inappropriate language).
- Do pray for them and yourself as you lead the group.
- Don't take favourites.

- Do not be physical with them (this can be misinterpreted).

Here are a few extra thoughts about keeping control to guide you:

The key to establishing good discipline and control is relationship building and clear expectations – these need to be thought through before MISSION:RESCUE starts.

This can be done by:

- Setting some ground rules and boundaries for the group – and sticking to them!
- Having plenty of materials for everyone.
- Ensuring you are fully prepared with everything you need to hand. Failure in this can open the door for behaviour problems!
- Ensuring that you have enough leaders at all times.
- Positively reinforcing the children's behaviour when they answer or do something well.
- Never sacrificing the needs of the group for one child.

For more information on leading small groups, check out
Top Tips on Leading small groups
SU, 978 1 84427 388 1
£3.50.

For more information on managing behaviour, see Top Tips on Handling difficult behaviour
SU, 978 1 84427 124 5
£3.50

PRAYING WITH CHILDREN

There will be many chances to pray with children during MISSION:RESCUE. There are two different aspects that come up during MISSION:RESCUE: praying about things with children and helping children make a response. There will be more about the latter in Session 2.

Praying with children

- Ask the children to name some of the things they want to pray for.
- Break these down into things they want to say sorry for, things they want to say thank you to God for, and things they want to ask for themselves or others.
- If you are going to lead the prayer yourself, make sure that you keep to the point and include the

suggestions the children made.

- Encourage the children, where possible, to lead the prayers with you.
- Be imaginative in using different ways to pray, eg using pictures or objects to stimulate thought; music to help praise or reflection; prayers with a set response; taking it in turns using one sentence; or prayers using different bodily postures. Suggestions are given each day for praying creatively.
- Take care to use simple, clear modern English, free from jargon, keeping it brief and relevant.

Talking with God should be very natural and the children need to realise this. Explain that we say 'Amen' as a means of saying we agree. We don't have to close our eyes and put our hands together!

For more information on praying with children, check out Top Tips on Prompting prayer
SU, 978 1 84427 322 5
£3.50.

READING THE BIBLE WITH CHILDREN

At MISSION:RESCUE we want children to understand that the Bible is God's Word for them today. It is important that the times when you read the Bible together are enjoyable and make sense to them! Children are not simply reading the Bible to get answers to our questions. Instead, we want their curiosity raised so that they can expect to meet God as they read the Bible, not just now, but in the future.

There will be much more about this in Session 3, but encourage your team between now and then to try to look at the Bible through the eyes of a child whenever they read it. What would a child find hard? What would they enjoy? What would they be most likely to remember from the passage? Just as children see the world at a different physical level, they often see spiritual things differently too, so encourage everyone to think from a child's perspective.

PRAYER

End your session with prayer for MISSION:RESCUE. Draw a large 'gingerbread' child on a sheet of paper; give out sticky notes and pens to everyone and invite them to write prayers on them that are about asking God to help you deal with the specific situations you have considered in this session: the programme, working with small groups, children with special needs or from other faith backgrounds. Then invite everyone to come in turn and stick their prayers on the shape, and to pray briefly either silently or aloud for those things.

SESSION 2
THE MISSION:RESCUE SPIRITUAL PROGRAMME

Use this session to focus the team's minds on spiritual preparation for the club.

WELCOME
Again, make sure you give the team a big welcome, ensuring refreshments are freely available, with the MISSION:RESCUE theme song playing in the background as people arrive.

WARM-UP GAME
Divide the group into teams of three or four and give each team a sheet of paper. They have three minutes in which to write down as many jobs that can be described as rescue work.

When you have done this, let each team in turn read out one of their roles; if others have it then everyone must cross it off their list. Keep going until every job has been read out, and applaud the team with the most roles still on their list!

THE CROSS WHERE JESUS DIED: GOD'S ULTIMATE MISSION:RESCUE
Throughout MISSION:RESCUE the children will be discovering how God rescued the Israelites from slavery in Egypt, especially through the escape from death (Day 4) and their escape through the sea (Day 5). On these two days the Bible material draws a parallel with Jesus as our rescuer. This Bible study is aimed at helping us understand how Jesus did this through his death on the cross: not the physical facts, but the spiritual work that God was doing through the events at Calvary.

Ask people to get into pairs and to tell each other a story of when they have been rescued from something, eg a breakdown in the car. Allow two minutes each for the storytelling! Then invite two or three people to tell the whole group what emotions they felt at the time and about the rescue.

It is often after events that we understand fully what has happened. By the time the apostle Paul was writing to young churches, Christians were beginning to understand the meaning of Jesus' death on the cross in

terms of four main ways: Jesus the sacrifice, Jesus the reconciler, Jesus the victor and Jesus the rescuer. It is this last understanding that will feature in MISSION: RESCUE.

Jesus the rescuer
In small groups, read Exodus 14:1–29 (and keep in mind the events of chapters 7–13) and discuss how God came to the rescue of the Israelites. What impact did his actions have on their situation?

Come back together and write up these findings on a flip chart.

Then read Romans 3:24 and Mark 10:45. Can you find parallels between the comments on the flip chart and what God did for people through Jesus' death on the cross?

The freeing of God's people from slavery in Egypt was a foretaste of what Jesus would do for all people through his death: Jesus rescued us from the power of evil and sin, from those things that stop us being the people we were made to be.

Read Luke 19:1–10. How did Jesus 'rescue' Zacchaeus? What did Jesus say was his mission (v 10)?

Children never find it easy to grasp timescales: what happened to you as a child could be, to them, in the same timeframe as what happened in the Bible. So be wise in the way your conversations with them jump from God's rescue of his people in Egypt to what happened when Jesus died on the cross! And yet it is important for them to grasp that what happened on the cross is still relevant to them today. Split into groups again and discuss the following questions, trying to think with the mind of a child:

- Who are today's 'rescuers'?
- In what situations today do people need to be rescued?
- If Jesus came to rescue people, what was he rescuing them from?

Come back together to share your answers. Remind people that children tend to think very literally and struggle with abstract concepts. The story of Dogger by Shirley Hughes (Red Fox, 2009) will be known to many children; you might want to read it to the group and talk about the way that rescue is portrayed in it. How does this relate to what Jesus did for us on the cross?

Pause, and pray for wisdom and skill in explaining these things to children.

FILE 3

Top Tips on
Explaining the cross
SU, 978 1 84427 330 0
£3.50

This book will equip church leaders and children's workers to explain the cross to children and young people so that they not only understand the richness of the message of the cross but are encouraged to respond. Four key ways to understand the cross are explored – Jesus takes our place, Jesus triumphs over evil, Jesus as a reconciler, Jesus' dramatic rescue bid. Full of inspiring stories and practical advice!

HELPING CHILDREN TO RESPOND

Much of the material you will cover in MISSION: RESCUE may prompt children to want to be friends with Jesus for themselves. Be ready to help them, but make sure that you stay within your church's child protection policy when praying with children.

- Unless you bring up the subject, a child may not have the words to begin a conversation about responding to Jesus. Explain that if at any time they do want to talk to you more, they should say 'Tell me more about Jesus', and then you will know what they want to discuss.
- They rarely need long explanations, just simple answers to questions.
- Talk to them in a place where you can be seen by others.
- Never put pressure on children to respond in a particular way, just help them take one step closer to Jesus when they are ready. We don't want them to respond just to please us!
- Treat each as an individual. So don't say, 'Hands up who wants to follow Jesus?' or make children say something that is not true for them, but allow each one to choose what is right for them.
- Always allow children a way out: give them an opportunity to go away and think about their decision and come back to you either later in the session or on the following day. This is God's work, and even if you don't have the chance to talk to them again he can actually achieve it without you!
- Remember, for many children there are a number of commitments as their understanding grows.
- Many children just need a bit of help to say what they want to say to God. On this page is a suggested prayer they could use to make a commitment to Jesus:

Jesus, I want to be your friend.
Thank you that you love me.
Thank you for living in the world and dying on a cross for me.
I'm sorry for all the wrong things I have done.
Please forgive me and let me be your friend.
Please let the Holy Spirit help me be like you.

Amen.

- Reassure them that God hears us when we talk with him and has promised to forgive us and help us to be his friends. Children need help to stick with Jesus, especially if their parents don't believe.
- Assure them that God wants to hear whatever they say. Give them some prayer ideas.
- Encourage them to keep coming to Christian activities, not necessarily on Sundays – their church might have to be the midweek club or a school lunch-time club.
- Reading the Bible will be easier with something like Snapshots – but you need to support them if they are to keep it up.
- Keep praying and maintain your relationship with them wherever possible.

Friends with Jesus (for 5 to 7s), Me+Jesus (for 8s and 9s) and Jesus=friendship forever will help to explain what it means to follow Jesus. Details are on the inside front cover.

For more information on helping children respond, see Top Tips on Helping a child respond to Jesus SU, 978 1 84427 387 4 £3.50.

WORKING WITH SPECIAL OR ADDITIONAL NEEDS

During MISSION:RESCUE you will face a number of challenges. Being prepared to take care of children with special or additional needs can be a tremendous blessing to both the children and their parents or carers. Here are a few guidelines for working with children with additional needs.

- Value every child as an individual. Before the start, find out as much as possible about them – their likes and dislikes, strengths and limitations. Then you will know how best to include them and make them feel safe.
- Prepare each session with a range of abilities in mind. Think carefully about working with abstract ideas. These may be misunderstood and taken literally! Have a range of craft ideas. Check that you do not give a child with learning difficulties a task that is appropriate for their reading age but inappropriate for their actual age. In other words, make sure that pictures and other aids are age-appropriate.
- Give all children opportunities to join in activities. Some children with additional needs may have distinctive areas of interest or talents that you can respond to. As far as possible, keep children with disabilities with their own peer group.
- If you have a child with a hearing impairment, make sure they sit near the front and that they can see the speaker's face clearly (not lit from behind). If a loop system is available, check that it is working for the child. Discussion in small groups can be hard for deaf children. Try to reduce background noise.
- Pay attention to any medical needs noted on the registration form, particularly any medication they take. Keep a record of any medication given, initialled by the first-aider and another team member.
- Designate leaders to work one-to-one with children with challenging behaviour. Where appropriate, set up a buddy system so that they work closely with a peer.
- Expect good behaviour from all children, but be tolerant of unusual behaviour. For example, some children need to fiddle with something in their hands. 'Concentrators' can be bought from www.tangletoys.com.
- Ensure that all the children know what is planned for the day. Some children will benefit from a schedule in words or symbols. Give the children a five-minute countdown when an activity is about to finish. Some children find any change of activity very difficult.

Top tips on Welcoming special children
SU, 978 1 84427 126 9
£3.50

Helping children with special needs to know God is challenging, but deeply rewarding. Find out what the Bible has to say on the subject and explore the implications of the Disability Discrimination Act for your church. Be encouraged and inspired with stories from group leaders and parents, and be equipped with lots of practical ideas for welcoming special children in your church and children's group.

WORKING WITH CHILDREN FROM OTHER FAITH BACKGROUNDS

Having children from different faiths come to our events is a great privilege. Knowing that their parents trust us to care for their children and are willing to allow us to share the good news of Jesus is exciting, but also gives us a responsibility to think about how we are going to treat the children and relate to their faith and culture. The principles below have been worked out by practitioners with many years experience of working in this context. Whilst you might not agree with all of them, we think they are worth serious consideration in order to ensure that we give a genuine welcome to children from other faith backgrounds. We have written these recognising that whilst some parents from different faiths are keen for their children to attend a club run by Christians, they might still have strong objections to their children becoming followers of Jesus. It is with this and other tensions in mind that we have produced these principles.

- We will not criticise, ridicule or belittle other religions.
- We will not tell the children what their faith says, nor define it by what some of its adherents do.
- We will not ask the children to say, sing or pray things that they do not believe, understand or that compromises their own faith.
- We will value and affirm the positive aspects of the children's culture.
- We will use music, artwork and methods that are culturally appropriate, for example Asian Christian music, pictures of people from a variety of backgrounds or single sex activities.
- We will be open and honest in our presentation of what Christians believe.
- We will be open and honest about the aims and content of our work with families, carers, teachers and other adults involved in their lives.

- We will seek to build long-term friendships that are genuine and which have no hidden agendas.
- We will relate to the children and young people within the context of their families and their families' belief system.
- We are committed to the long-term nature of the work, for the children now and the impact this could have on future generations.
- Where children show a desire to follow Jesus we will discuss the issues surrounding such a course of action, particularly relating to honouring and obeying parents. We will be honest about the consequences following Jesus might have for them.
- We will never suggest that the children keep things secret from their families or carers.
- We seek to promote mutual respect between diverse groups and encourage community cohesion.

Top Tips on Welcoming children of other faiths
SU, 978 1 84427 250 1
£3.50

What does the Bible say about those of other faiths and how we should live out our faith amongst them? What can your church do? Here's a readable and practical guide which will inspire and equip you to build relationships with children and their families. It's packed with practical, fun ideas that will strengthen or even kick-start your ministry with those of other faiths.

If you expect to have children from other faith backgrounds attending, remind your team of the importance of treating the Bible as a holy book: never simply put it down on the floor, but always place it carefully on a table (and especially don't use it to raise the height of a projector, for example!). Be sure that you use copies that are in good condition, as one which is falling apart would be shameful to some children from other faith backgrounds.

If you are serving food at any activities, check that it will be appropriate for any child from another faith background.

PRAYER

Spend some time together as a team praying for each other, for MISSION:RESCUE and for all the children who will come.

It would be great to get the leaders of each Spy Ring to pray together. You may wish to use some of the creative prayer ideas you will find in each day's session outlines.

Or find some silhouettes of children, preferably of a boy and a girl, and print off enough for everyone to have one of each. Use the silhouettes to pray for the children who will come: they may be unknown to you, but God knows their names and all their needs. Ask him to be at work in each child. Encourage the team to take home their silhouettes and pray for the children regularly. You may even want to turn them in to fridge magnets – print on card and stick magnetic tape on the back – so that they are in a prominent place. (But do not include any child's name on anything that the team will take home with them.)

Pray too for the team by having all of those with each role stand whilst you pray for them and their work during MISSION:RESCUE. Ask God to fill each one with his Holy Spirit to make them more like Jesus and to skill them for the tasks he has given them.

SESSION 3
USING THE BIBLE WITH CHILDREN

This training feature is available on the DVD and at www.scriptureunion.org.uk/missionrescue

You may also find these Top Tips books helpful:

Top Tips on Sharing Bible stories
SU, 978 1 84427 328 7 £3.50

Top Tips on Communicating God in non-book ways
SU, 978 1 84427 329 4 £3.50

Top Tips on Discovering the Bible with children
SU, 978 1 84427 335 5 £3.50

FILE 4

Q-Tech's spy store

In Q-Tech's spy store you'll find many of the resources you need for MISSION:RESCUE: craft and game ideas including templates, code sheets, the theme song and 'Who's the Mole' drama. You can photocopy those pages marked 'Photocopiable'. For Bible discovery notes as single sheets, the Learn and remember verse sheet music, more codes and any other resources go to www.scriptureunion.org.uk/missionrescue.

Construction/craft

Use some of these construction (craft) activities during Q-Tech's workshop, choosing an individual or an all-together construction.

BIBLE-THEMED CRAFT

MOSES BASKETS
What you need
- [ ] Card (A5 size)
- [ ] Strips of card (6 cm x 1 cm)
- [ ] Strips of coloured paper (1 cm strips cut lengthways from A4)
- [ ] Sticky tape
- [ ] Pencils
- [ ] Scissors

What you do
Give the children a sheet of A5 card. Encourage them to stick the strips of card around the edge, at intervals of 2 or 3 centimetres. Turn over the basket base and bend the strips of card up, so that they stand up. (For younger groups, you could do this part of the construction before the session, so that they can start straight on the next step.)

Weave strips of coloured paper through these strips of card to form the sides of the basket. To make it easier, tape the end of each coloured strip to one of the card strips. This will hold it in place as you weave. Trim and tape down the ends of each of the strips when you have finished each level of weave. While you work, chat about the Bible story you have explored and, if you wish, encourage the children to write their thoughts on the coloured strips, before they weave them into their basket.

SNAKE WALKING STICKS
What you need
- [ ] Strips of brown paper (1 cm strips cut lengthways from A4)
- [ ] Small squares of brown paper (about 4 cm x 4 cm)
- [ ] Piece of bamboo cane or dowelling (about 28 to 30 cm long)
- [ ] Sticky tape
- [ ] Sticky tack
- [ ] Felt-tip pens
- [ ] Scissors

What you do
Give each child four strips of paper. Show them how to stick two strips together end to end to make a longer strip. Do this with the other two strips as well. Then tape the end of one strip on top of the end of the other, at right angles. Start to fold the strip underneath across the top of the upper strip. Continue to do so, folding the lower strip across the top of the upper strip, so that you form a kind of concertina. When you have come to the ends of the strip, tape those ends together. Open out the concertina as far as it will go.

On the square of paper, draw a snake's head and cut it out. Stick it to one end of the concertina to form a complete snake. Then stick the head end of your snake to one end of the cane or dowel and wind the body of the snake round the cane. Stick the 'tail' to the other end of the cane, using sticky tack so that it can be taken off easily.

The children should have a miniature snake staff. They can turn it into a snake by unfastening the tail end, and using the cane to make the snake move about. Sticking the tail back to the cane again will turn the snake back into a staff!

SALT DOUGH MODELLING
What you need
- [ ] 300 g plain flour
- [ ] 300 g salt
- [ ] 15 ml cooking oil
- [ ] 200 ml water

What you do
Measure out the ingredients into a large mixing bowl and mix well together. Add a little extra water if the dough is too dry. Tip the dough on to a floured surface. Knead well. When the dough is smooth and feels springy, it is ready to use.

If you don't want to prepare the dough with the children, but just do the modelling activity, prepare the dough before the session, as above, and give each child a piece of dough to work with. However, preparing the dough together will enable you to talk to the children about the punishment Pharaoh gave the Israelites because of what Moses asked – to make bricks without straw. Salt dough items can be cooked to make them hard. Place them on a greased baking tray in the centre of an oven. Cook at a low temperature. Larger and thicker items will take several hours.

Encourage the children to make a model, perhaps from the story. If you want to link it closely to the story, ask the children to make individual bricks, and then use them to build something such as the doorway to an Egyptian temple or a pyramid!

Let the dough dry – it will need leaving overnight. If you wish, you can use another construction session to paint the models.

FLATBREAD MAKING
What you need
- [ ] One cup flour
- [ ] ⅓ cup water
- [ ] Salt
- [ ] Olive oil
- [ ] Baking sheets
- [ ] Rolling pins
- [ ] Fork
- [ ] Wire rack
- [ ] Access to an oven (and an adult to use it)

What you do
Preheat the oven to 220 °C/gas mark 7, and place the baking sheets inside to heat up. Work together in groups of no more than six children with an adult to make the dough and roll it out. Make sure you involve the children at every step. Put the flour into a bowl and add a pinch of salt. Gradually add the water to the flour, stirring quickly with a fork. When you have some dough, form it into a ball. Dust a work surface and the rolling pins with flour. Divide the dough into four to six pieces. Flatten the ball between your hands and place on the floured surface.

Roll each piece into a 12 to 13 cm circle. Then roll them further, into 20 cm pancakes. (It is important to allow the dough to rest between rollings.) Prick the dough with a fork. Remove the preheated baking sheets and place the dough pancakes onto the sheets. Bake for 2 minutes on each side, until the bread is lightly brown and crisp. Transfer to a wire rack and allow to cool. Sprinkle with olive oil to taste.

As you work together, chat about the story and how the Israelites use flatbread to celebrate Passover. What can the children remember about Passover?

PILLARS
What you need
- [ ] Two cardboard tubes per child
- [ ] Glue
- [ ] Cotton wool
- [ ] Grey paint and paintbrushes
- [ ] Red, yellow and orange paper
- [ ] Scissors

What you do
Remind children that God went with the Israelites, by day as a pillar of cloud and by night as a pillar of fire. Give each child two cardboard tubes. Show them how to stick cotton wool onto one tube to form the pillar of cloud. Dab grey paint on the pillar to create a more cloud-like appearance.

Then cut out flame shapes from the red, yellow and orange paper, and stick these to the other cardboard tube, to form the pillar of fire. Overlap the different colours to give the impression of raging fire!

As you work, chat about the story – how God rescued the Israelites by separating the sea to form a path, and how God was with the Israelites all the time. Chat about how we can know that God is with us too. In what situations would the children especially want God to be with them? Encourage the children to take their pillars home to remind them that God is always with them and wants to rescue them too.

SPY-THEMED CRAFT

DISGUISES

What you do
- [ ] Paper and card of different colours
- [ ] Templates from page 33/website
- [ ] Wool of different colours
- [ ] Glue
- [ ] Felt-tip pens
- [ ] Sticky tape

What you need

To make a beard, give out paper and the beard templates and encourage the children to draw around the template and cut it out. Ask the children to choose an appropriate colour of wool and to cut it into short lengths. Spread glue on the beard shape and stick the wool down. Make sure they cover the paper well to give a convincing beard texture! Stick a length of wool to either side of the beard and tie these round the child's head to attach the beard.

To make glasses, draw round the template onto a dark-coloured piece of paper. Give the children the chance to customise the basic glasses shape by adding on extra bits, making them square or a horn-rimmed shape! Cut out the glasses and help the children put them on.

How well can the children change their appearance? You could finish with a disguise fashion show!

POTATO SECRET WRITING

What you need
- [ ] Potatoes
- [ ] Spoon and table knife
- [ ] Plain matchsticks (available from craft shops)
- [ ] Paper
- [ ] Access to an oven (and an adult to use it)

What you do

Before the session, create the potato inkwells. Chop a potato in half, and scoop a small well out of the cut side with a spoon. Then scrape the blade of a table knife across the cut side, to squeeze potato juice into the well. Put a matchstick in the well, ready for the children to use.

Give out sheets of paper and encourage the children to write a message on the paper, using the matchstick and potato juice. They could write a message, draw a map, or draw a description of an enemy spy. If they like, they can do more than one secret message.

When you have all finished, put the papers into a warm oven (120–130 °C, gas mark ½) for a few minutes. This will reveal the secret message or picture.

Other inks you could use are lemon juice, milk, onion juice and cola. Why not use all of these and compare which one gives the best results? What would come out top in your spy experiment?

SEMAPHORE FLAGS

What you need
- [ ] A4 sheets of coloured paper
- [ ] Lengths of bamboo cane or dowelling (around 30 cm long)
- [ ] Sticky tape
- [ ] Felt-tip pens
- [ ] Collage materials and glue (optional)
- [ ] Semaphore alphabet from the MISSION:RESCUE website

What you do

Give each child two sheets of paper and two lengths of cane or dowel. Encourage the children to decorate their paper any way they like. They may like to put their names, the name of their team, or a secret message written in code – it's up to them how they personalise the paper. If you have them available, they could use collage materials, as well as felt-tip pens. Make sure they leave a gap of about 2 cm down one of the short sides of the paper. When everyone has finished both sheets, tape the blank short side of the paper to the cane to form a semaphore flag.

When everyone has two complete flags, you could teach the children how to communicate using their flags by using the semaphore alphabet from the MISSION: RESCUE website. Can you create a special message that the children can send and understand?

GADGET MAKING (JUNK MODELLING)

What you need
- [ ] 'Junk' such as cereal boxes, egg boxes, bottle tops, tin foil, sweet wrappers, crisp tubes, yogurt pots, cardboard tubes
- [ ] Glue and masking tape
- [ ] Marker pens, paint and paintbrushes
- [ ] Scissors

What you do

Encourage the children to create a spy gadget from the junk that you have collected together. They could create a scanning device, a telescope, binoculars or a mini-computer – let them use their imagination, but try to steer them away from guns! Work together to produce the various spy devices. When you have finished the construction of the devices, paint your models to make them more convincing! When everything is painted and dried, exhibit your devices to the rest of the club.

Masking tape is suggested here, as it is easier to paint over than sticky tape.

SECRET PICTURES (WAX PICTURES)
What you need
- [ ] Large sheets of white paper
- [ ] White candles
- [ ] Poster paint of various colours (watered down)

What you do

Encourage the children to draw a picture on the paper with the white candles. This will be their secret picture, as it won't show on the paper as they are drawing it. They could write a message, or a logo for their team, or copy the MISSION:RESCUE logo – let them use their imaginations as to what to draw.

When everyone has finished their picture, show them how to paint the paper to reveal the picture. The paint sticks to the paper, but is repelled by the wax. They could use stripes of different coloured paint to make their picture more interesting.

To take this further, you could get children to draw another picture, but then swap with another child before they start to paint. How many can guess what this new picture is or decipher the message as they paint over it?

Games

RESCUE-THEMED GAMES
All these games include the idea of rescue, to help you reinforce the message of MISSION:RESCUE!

PARACHUTE GAMES (SHARKS)
What you need
- [ ] Parachute

What you do

Choose one child to be the shark and two players to be lifeguards. Everyone else sits holding the edge of the parachute, with their legs underneath. The shark goes underneath the parachute and tries to pull children underneath the parachute by their legs. The lifeguards have to patrol the edge of the parachute, and rescue those children who are being pulled under by pulling them out. It is important that you referee this game carefully, so that children aren't the victim of a tug of war between the lifeguard and the shark! Be quick to judge if a child has been rescued or pulled under, so that no one gets hurt. Once a player has been pulled under the parachute, they become a shark too. The winner is either the last player to be pulled under, or you could time how long the lifeguards can keep everyone safe, before swapping lifeguards.

STUCK IN THE MUD
What you do

The traditional game of 'stuck in the mud' illustrates the idea of rescue very well. Choose one or two children to be 'on'. They have to chase and tag other children. Once tagged, a child has to stand still, with feet apart and arms out wide. Another player can rescue them if they either run under an outstretched arm or crawl between their legs. (If you are playing this outside, running under outstretched arms is better, as children won't hurt their knees or get muddy.) Once everyone is stuck in the mud, change the children who are 'on'.

DISCOVER THE MESSAGE/
CAPTURE THE GADGET
What you need
- [ ] Short lengths of wool in two different colours
- [ ] A secret message or a spy gadget for each team

What you do

Split the children into two teams (you could group a number of Spy Rings together) and assign a part of your playing space as each team's base. Place their message or gadget in their base. Tie a length of wool loosely round the wrist of each child, and give some spare lengths to a leader, who should stay at the team base at all times.

The children should try to capture the message or gadget of the opposing team and bring it back to their own base, before being caught by the opposing team. If a child is caught by a member of the other team, they should surrender the wool on their wrist to the opposing player and return to their own base for a new length of wool. The winner is the team that captures the opposing team's message/gadget first. You could award extra points in the game for the most amount of wool captured from the other team.

This works best in a large area, either outside or played throughout a building. Try to have team bases that are hidden from each other. Ideally, each team should start out not knowing where the opposing team's base is. Risk assess this carefully, and make sure your playing area is free from hazards. Have team members around if children have to go up and down stairs, and be on hand to solve any disputes about who caught who! Carefully planned, this game is a real winner!

BALL-GAME RESCUE

What you need

☐ Large sponge ball
☐ Masking tape or chalk

What you do

Mark out your playing area. Divide the area into two, and mark a line down the middle. Then at the back of each half, mark off a narrow strip – this is the prison!

Spilt the children into two teams (or play a round robin-style tournament between Spy Rings), with one team starting in each half. The object is to throw the ball at the opposing team and hit one of the opposition (not on the head). The 'hit' player then goes and stands in the prison behind the opposition half. If the opposing team catches or avoids the ball, they are not out, and get to throw the ball back at the first team. The winning team is the one that has put all the opposing players into their prison.

However, a player in prison can free themselves by gathering the ball (either because it has evaded the opposing team or their own team has thrown it directly to them) and hitting one of the opposition. If they do this, they return to their own half and the player they hit has to go to prison.

BALL POOL RESCUE

What you need

☐ Paddling pool
☐ Ball-pool balls
☐ Gunge (or water)
☐ Toy fishing nets

What you do

Before the session, fill the paddling pool with gunge (or water for a simpler game). Put the balls into the pool, pushing them into the gunge.

Split the children into two teams (or do this in Spy Rings) and line them up at one end of the room, with the gunge pool and fishing nets at the other end. In turn, the children have to run to the pool, pick up a fishing net and rescue a ball from the gunge. When they have pulled one out, they run back to their team, and the next player goes. The winning team is the one with the most balls at the end of an allotted time.

If you are using water, the balls will float on the top. You could make this more difficult by adding other floating things to the pool to act as decoys (such as rubber ducks, boats – anything that floats!).

SPY-THEMED GAMES

Carry on your spy theme by using these espionage games!

SPY RELAY RACES

What you need

☐ Any items for your chosen relay race

What you do

Organise some relay races that emphasise your spy theme. You could try:

- **Evidence sorting**: cut up some pictures of the leaders (such as Agents X and Y, the Chief or the Head of Security). Make sure you have a set of pictures per Spy Ring. Mix up the pieces and put them at one end of the room, opposite each team of children. In turn, the children have to run to one end of the room, pick up a piece of the jigsaw and bring it back. Another child collects a piece and so on. The winning team is the one that has put together all their jigsaws.

- **Secret messages**: Before the session, prepare a list of five or six secret messages, either spy-themed or about the day's story. Spread the Spy Rings out into lines. On a given signal, the first child in each line is shown the message. They have to then whisper it once to the next person in their team and so on, with the last player writing down what they think the message was. Once all the messages have been passed down the line, check to see which team has the most messages correct.

- **Disguises**: At one end of the room, have a pile of dressing up clothes that could be used for disguises (hats, coats, scarves, sunglasses, false facial hair etc). In turn, each child runs to the pile of clothes, selects one and then runs back. They should then dress one of their Spy Ring in this piece of clothing, while another player runs to collect another item of clothing and so on. When all the clothing is gone, decide who the best disguised spy is!

EVIDENCE HUNT

What you need

☐ A list of 15 to 20 items the children need to collect

What you do

Split the children into teams (or compete in Spy Rings) and give each team a copy of the list. Set the boundaries of your search area and send the teams off to find all the items on the list. Give the teams a time limit (depending on the complexity of the list and the size of your playing area), and see how many objects the teams can collect before the time is up. Count up the objects at the end – the team with the most objects is the winner.

Alternatively, you could ask each team to find one thing that begins with each letter of the alphabet (apple, beech leaf, crayon etc). To make this easier, you might decide to allow the teams to take pictures of the items, rather than collect them up (make sure each team has a digital camera or camera phone).

PICTURE CHALLENGE

What you need
- [ ] 'Distorted' pictures of the leaders
- [ ] Baby photos of the leaders
- [ ] Photos of the leaders' parents

What you do
Before the session, collect together and print out pictures in the above categories (there are various pieces of software and websites that will allow you to distort pictures – some mobile phones will also do it). In one area, stick up all your distorted photos, in another all the baby photos and in a third area all the pictures of parents.

Challenge the Spy Rings to go round and identify the 'distorted' leaders, decide which leader is the baby in each photo and which leader each set of parents belongs to. To make it easier, you could include a list of names for the children to choose from. Can the children crack these clues?

(As well as pictures, you could use the fingerprints or footprints of various leaders.)

BOMB DEFUSAL

What you need
- [ ] Balloons (preferably black)
- [ ] Small slips of paper
- [ ] Pen

What you do
Try one of these bomb-game variations!
- **Bomb mania**: Before the session, blow up lots of balloons. Challenge the children to pop as many balloons as they can in 20 seconds. This of course requires a lot of balloons and will be very noisy, but most children will think that it's great fun.
- **Bomb disposal**: Before the session, write 'Bomb defused!' on most of the slips of paper, and on the remaining slips, write 'Bomb exploded!'. Blow up the balloons and put one of the slips of paper into each balloon. Challenge the children to pop one balloon at a time. They should read the paper inside and see if they managed to defuse the bomb, or whether it

has exploded! If they find an exploded message, they have to stop. If they find a defused message, they pop another balloon and so one until they find an exploded message. How many bombs were defused? There will be children that don't like popping balloons, so make sure you have somewhere quiet for them to go (and something for them to do) while this game is taking place.

OBSERVATION SKILLS

What you need
- [ ] A clip of an appropriate film (such as one of the Spy Kids films or The Spy Next Door)
- [ ] List of questions about the film clip
- [ ] TV and DVD player/laptop and projector

What you do
Before the session, watch your selected clip and come up with some questions about the clip. Make sure you include some more obvious questions, so that most children will get some right, then include some more obscure ones, about smaller details of the clip.

Tell the children that you're going to show a film clip, and then ask questions about details in the clip afterwards. The children have to use their skills of observation to try to notice as much as they can. Show the film clip to the children and then go on to ask your questions. You could do this in Spy Rings or individually. Once you have finished, reveal the answers – the Spy Ring/individual with the most correct answers is the winner!

These films have a PG certificate and if you feel that showing excerpts may be a concern to the parents, do inform them in advance. Also check your church has a licence to show films. Go to www.ccli.co.uk/licences/churches_showing-films.cfm for further information on this.

BEARD AND SPECTACLES TEMPLATE

For use with the craft activity 'Disguises' on page 29.

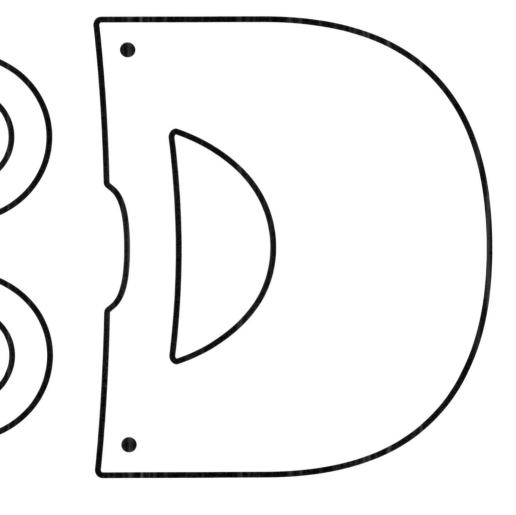

Hieroglyph messages

MESSAGE 1

MESSAGE 2

KEYCODE

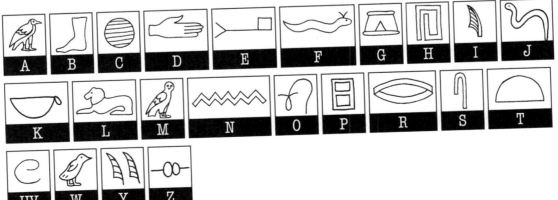

FOR USE IN MISSION 4

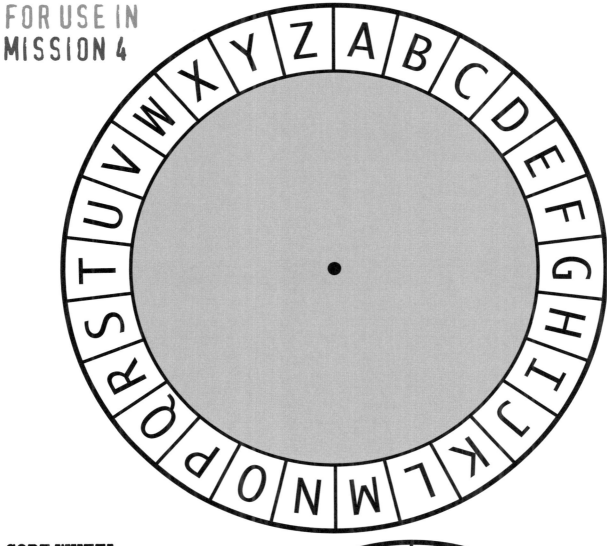

CODE WHEEL

How to use

- Cut out the two circles.
- Fasten the two wheels together with a split pin.
- Use the outer wheel for plain alphabet and the inner wheel for the code alphabet.

Crack the code

CK GXK YKIXKZ GMKTZY

and then make up code messages for others to crack.

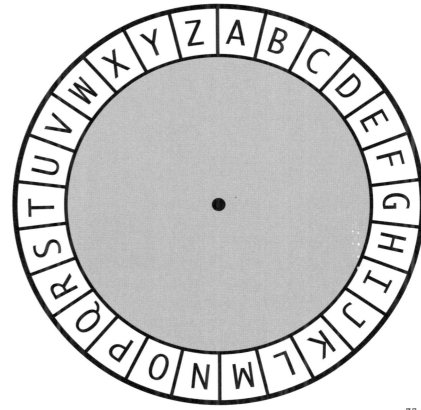

FILE 4

The MISSION:RESCUE theme song

Alex Taylor
Arr. Ruth Wills

DRAMA
Who's the mole?

CHARACTERS

Agent M – team leader, likes to think he knows what he's doing. Is oftenover-confident and has an overly 'heroic' way of speaking.

Agent O – second in command, really knows what's going on. Is practical and spends most of her time mopping up after M.

Agent S – the boffin of the group is in charge of the technological side of things. Often no one understands what he says!

Agent E – the accident-prone idiot of the group. Only got through spy training by copying from other students.

Agent Z – the mole, is outwardly helpful and kind, but sabotages the group's plans at every chance. She reveals her plans to the audience alone.

Chief – the head spy appears in the first and last episode. Should have a cut-glass English accent!

Two or three **accomplices** for Agent Z on Day 5 – dressed all in black, these are non-speaking roles.

These roles can be played by either sex, but the doctoring of the messages is easier if Z is female.

Mission 1
Raid by enemy agents

PROPS
- Technical equipment/TV screen
- Torch
- Some kind of hand-held gadget
- Heroic music
- Giant sandwich
- Table, chair
- Map
- Mugs
- Mobile phone
- Sound effects of sirens and helicopters (optional)

Scene: a secret meeting place, dark and mysterious, there are screens and technical 'equipment' around the place that Agent S is in control of (throughout the episode, he should work on the equipment as if he knows what it does). The meeting place is empty to start.

Agent O comes on stealthily, shining a torch everywhere, checking for enemy agents. She turns and backs further on stage. At the same time, Agent S comes on backwards, closely examining a hand-held gizmo. They back into each other. S screams and drops his gadget.

Agent O: WHO GOES THERE! WHO DO YOU WORK FOR?

Agent S screams again and picks up his gadget. Looking at the screen he suddenly recognises who it is.

Agent S: Oh, Agent O, it's you.

O: No, not U, O.

S: What? No, you are O, aren't you?

O: No, I'm not R or U. Just Agent O.

S: Eh?

O: And I'm not Agent A either, a bit big-headed, that Agent A.

S: What?

O: How did you know it was me?

S: My UVU detected your mobile and informed me of your identity.

O: Your what?

S: My Undercover Verification Unit. It has all the profiles of the agents assigned to this mission.

O: Oh, goodie. Well, let's see who's on the team.

S: Well, it says that our leader is Agent M.

O: (Obviously disappointed at this, she sighs heavily.) Oh—

S: (Interrupting.) No, not you: Agent M.

O: What? Er… No, I was just about to say—

Agent M: (Marching heroically into the room.) Don't worry, team, I'm here! We can start the mission now! And I can assure you that you can count on my bravery, strength, cunning, intelligence and extreme—

O: Big-headedness?

M: What? Oh, hello, O! How are you? I bet you've missed me, haven't you?

O: Like a hole in the head. M, this is Agent S. Seems like he's the technician on the team.

S: Pleased to meet you, M.

M: So are we all here?

S: No, apparently there are two more agents to arrive. (Tapping buttons on his gadget.) Agent E—

Agent E: (Entering eating a giant sandwich, he speaks with his mouth full.) Hmwnirg ealr ugawegrhwh gg.

M: (Leaping into action.) He's obviously speaking in code. S, what do you make of it?

O: M—

E: (Still eating.) Hmreogi wskrjg ehgaheguawb.

M: Quick S, this could be important!

O: (Trying to get his attention.) M!

M: Quiet O, this could be news of our mission. (Becoming wistful. If possible, heroic music can he heard in the background. E and S look incredulous; O looks a bit cheesed off.) What heroic deeds will I be called on to perform next? How will I be able to show my bravery? In what marvellous ways will I be able to inspire my fellow agents?

O: (Shouting.) M! (Music abruptly stops.)

M: What?

O: I think he's just speaking with his mouth full.

E: Wotcha! Sorry about that. My mum always told me not to chat while eating. E's the name, spying's the game. (He shakes S's hand, and S realises he has now got bits of E's sandwich all over his fingers.)

S: Er, pleased to meet you, I think…

M: So S, my technological boffin of a spy friend, is there anyone else on the team?

S: Yes, just one more, but my Undercover Verification Unit is having trouble displaying the profile – it seems to be corrupted.

Agent Z: (Arriving stealthily, she greets the other agents with fake sincerity.) I'm Agent Z, lovely to meet you – I've just been transferred from Spy HQ. M, what a great pleasure, I've heard so much about you! Agent O, always good to meet an agent of such quality. S, a technological genius. And E… (She looks at him and then walks back to M, seeming to have decided not to waste any time on E.)

M: Agent Z, eh? Don't think I've worked with you, have I? But you obviously know me and that's the most important thing, eh, O? (He slaps O on the back.)

O: What? (Sarcastically.) Oh yes, of course.

At this point, the Chief appears. He can either do this in person, or appear in a pre-recorded film on one of the TVs on the set. The Chief (or the TV screen) is stage left. The team line up in the order M, O, S, E and Z from left to right, with M nearest the Chief/screen.

Chief: Greetings, team. Now that you're all here, let's get straight down to business. I've gathered you together because the secret papers on Operation Moses Rescue have been stolen! This vital information has been telling us all about God's rescue mission thousands of years ago, and what it means today. But now those papers have been stolen, we can't discover any more. It is vitally important that you find these papers! We'll be passing on information and all our leads to you, so you'll need to put together all the clues to crack this case. Can I count on you?

M: You sure can, Chief. I've been on hundreds of missions—

O: (Stage whisper to the audience.) Yes, a few of them were even successful!

M: (Carrying on regardless.) And you can be sure that we'll catch the perpetrators and retrieve the papers.

Chief: Good, M. Right there's no time to lose! Get going!

The Chief either strides off or the TV goes black.

M: Right team, let's get to it! S, you calibrate your instruments; O, get the maps and spy satellite photographs, Z, fire up the codebreaking machines and E… you get the tea.

O: What are you going to do?

M: I'm going to think about the case! (He sits on a chair and strikes a heroic, thoughtful pose.) Well, off you go!

O, S, E and Z rush about the stage. There is much crashing into each other, with maps being dropped, equipment being sat on, tea cups being dropped. E goes offstage to make the tea. Finally O rolls out a map on the table. M, S and Z join her looking at the map.

O: So we're here, and the papers were last seen over here.

E: (Coming back on stage.) E-up! Tea's up! (He puts the tea heavily down on the map and the mugs fall over.)

O: E, that's gone all over the map!

S: And some of my equipment!

There is a lot of shouting, and discussion on who's to blame and who needs to clear up the mess. During this noise, Z creeps away and takes out her mobile phone. While the others are still arguing, she stage whispers into the phone.

Z: Yes, I've fooled them. They don't know I'm a mole! They think I'm a secret agent too! Targets are at the secret meeting place; they don't suspect a thing. Go! Go! Go!

Immediately, there are bangs and crashes offstage. If you can get sound effects of sirens and helicopters, all the better!

Offstage voice: Secret agents, you're surrounded!

O: Oh no! Our cover's been blown. How did they find us?

E and M: (Panicking and running around in circles.) We're doomed, we're doomed! ARGH!

O: We've got to get out of here!

S starts gathering up equipment. O pulls out a mobile and speaks into it.

O: Chief, where's the nearest safe house? (She pauses; there is still banging and crashing.) Thanks! (She puts away mobile, then speaks to others.) It's three streets away!

Z: (Shocked.) I didn't know about the safe house...

O: Come on, let's go!

O grabs M and E, who are still gibbering and panicking, and drags them off. S follows carrying as many gadgets as he can. Z follows slowly after them.

Z: (Leaving.) They didn't tell me there was a safe house...

Mission 2
Beware! There's a mole

PROPS
- Clown outfit
- Piece of paper
- Chair
- False beard and sunglasses

The scene is different from yesterday, but this can be achieved by moving some of the props around – nothing new needs to be introduced. The agents all enter, chatting about the raid by enemy agents. Agent Z is joining in, not letting on that she arranged the raid.

O: How did they find us? All the information was top secret!

S: Everything was encrypted with a code I invented myself.

M: Well, thanks to me, we're all safe. My instincts and training kicked in and I made sure that all my team were safe.

O: (Looking at him in disbelief.) What?

M: No need to thank me, just doing my job.

E: So where are we?

O: A safe house – a hideout that not many people know about. We should be OK for a while.

M: OK, everyone, get everything ready. I need to sit and think things through. (He sits down, closes his eyes as if thinking, and promptly starts snoring.)

S: I'll set up the equipment and then we can start processing the information. (He starts messing with gadgets, plugging things in etc, using whatever props you have.)

O: So, we need to gather some information. E, you'll need to go out in disguise to meet a contact.

E: Master of disguise, me! (He disappears to get changed.)

Z: What do we know so far?

O: Not much at the moment – just that the papers were stolen two nights ago from Spy HQ – that's where you used to work, isn't it, Z?

Z: (Struggling to come up with an excuse.) Er, well, um... I wasn't there... I've been on holiday... yes, for a month. I went to, er... Belgium.

O: Belgium?

Z: Yes, Belgium. I... er... I'm a big fan of, um... (Slowly, ashamed that this is the best she can come up with.) Belgian waffles.

O: (Thinking Z is a bit weird.) Right.

S: Incoming message!

O: Excellent, what does it say?

S: It's from Agent G, but it's in code. I'll feed it into my codebreaker and set it to work. (Z goes over to S to 'help'.)

E: (Coming on dressed as a clown.) Will this do?

O: What's that?!

E: I'm a clown. Smell this flower.

O smells the flower and water squirts out of it, into her face.

O: E, that's not what I meant. When you're in disguise, no one's meant to notice you. Oh, never mind, I'll go. (She goes offstage muttering to herself.)

M: (Waking up and seeing E dressed as a clown.) AAAARRRRGGGHH!! Mummy! It's the evil clown! (He runs and hides behind Z.)

E: What's up with him?

S: It would seem our leader is a sufferer of coulrophobia.

M: Mummy!

E: What-a-phobia?

S: He's scared of clowns.

E: Oh! It's OK, M, it's only me!

He takes off his wig to show M, but this only makes M more scared. He runs across the stage, and E chases him.

E: Come back, M, don't be scared.

E continues to chase M around the stage, leaping over the set and falling over props. Eventually they are interrupted by S.

S: Incoming message! It's a carrier pigeon!

Z: I'll catch it. (**Looking up to the ceiling.**) Here birdie, birdie! Come to Auntie Z!

At this point, the imaginary bird 'poos' on Z. Z can either pretend, or if you have the facilities, you could rig up a way to drop white 'goo' at the appropriate time.

Z: Eurgh! Disgusting bird.

E: (**Picking up a piece of paper from behind a nearby chair.**) Well, at least it dropped its message.

M: (**Still nervous of the clown outfit.**) OK, E, you read that and I'll get back to my thinking. (**He sits down again and goes back to sleep.**)

E: (**Opening the pigeon message and reading it.**) 'Beware!...'

E is interrupted by a 'Ping' noise from one of S's gadgets.

S: Agent G's message has been decoded. I'll print it out. (**He disappears offstage to get the printout.**)

E: 'Beware! There is a mole. Identity unknown. Mole is female.' What's a mole?

Z suddenly looks very worried. Shakily, she takes the note message from E.

Z: Let me see that...

O comes back in, wearing a false beard and sunglasses.

O: I got the message from our contact. Here's what it says—

E: Lovely beard, O, can I try it on?

O takes it off and gives it to E, who puts it on.

S: (**Coming back on with printout.**) Here's Agent G's decoded message.

Z: Let me see! (**She takes it from S and reads it quietly to herself, so that the children can hear the message. The other agents move to look at M, in disbelief that he's asleep again.**) 'Enemy agents are hiding at the petrol station.' Oh no!

M suddenly wakes up, sees E wearing the beard and screams.

E: What now?

S: It looks like M also has pogonophobia – the fear of beards.

M runs off, being chased by E. S and O follow trying to stop E and calm M down. In the ensuing chaos Z starts tearing holes in the two messages she has. Eventually O has enough and stops.

O: (**Shouting.**) EVERYONE STOP NOW!

Everyone freezes where they are. E should be in a silly position, lose his balance and fall over.

O: Z, give me those messages, we must find out where we should go. (**Z gives her the messages and O opens them so that the children can see. The two Z had are now full of holes.**) Z, what happened?

Z: (**Frantically trying to think of an excuse.**) Er... Mice!

O: What?

Z: Yes... a giant mouse came and started to eat the messages.

I managed to fight it off with my expert self-defence skills and rescue the notes, but not before it chewed holes in them. Don't worry, they still make sense!

O: (**Not sure she believes Z, but carrying on.**) OK. My message says, 'Enemy agents are moving on at 13.00 hours.' That's in an hour! Agent G's message reads, 'Enemy agents are hiding at the station.' And the last one says, 'Beware! There is a mole. Identity unknown. Mole is male.' A mole! Someone's trying to ruin our mission! (**She looks at M, E and S suspiciously.**) Which one of you is it?

Z: O, we've not got much time to lose – we need to get to the station! We can unmask the mole when we've completed the mission.

O: You're right, Z, no time to lose (**Turning to the men.**) But I'm watching you...

M, O, S and E leave the stage, arguing about who the mole is. Z is left behind.

Z: (**Laughing evilly.**) Ha, ha, ha! They've fallen for my trick! They'll never get the secret papers back! Now I just need to contact my agents to come and steal all this equipment. (**She leaves to the boos of the audience.**)

Mission 3
Capturing enemy agents

PROPS
- Plant pots
- Benches
- Rubbish bins
- Walkie-talkies
- Spy equipment
- Large piece of cloth

The scene at the front of the stage is a train station, so you can dress the stage as simply or as ornately as you like. You could use sound effects to create the impression of the station. Make sure you have some things (plant pots, benches or rubbish bins) for the agents to hide behind. The agents come on stage through the children so make sure they can do so safely. All the agents have walkie-talkies and a range of spy equipment. Much of this episode relies on the agents moving through the hall stealthily – the stage directions are suggestions on how you could perform the episode, but use your hall and set up as creatively as you can.

O: (Creeping on first, speaking into walkie-talkie.) O to M, all clear. The children are here, but as long as they stay back, they won't be harmed. You can stay out of our way, can't you, children?

The children shout their answer.

M: (Striding on, with no pretence of trying to be undercover.) Good work, O. (Heroic music starts in the background.) Just think, O – this could be my most heroic mission of all time. Imagine, recapturing the Operation Moses Rescue papers single-handedly. Battling through enemy agents, rescuing my team—

O: (In a loud whisper.) M! Sssshhh! We're meant to be undercover! And what do you mean single-handedly?

M: (Slapping O on the back.) Of course, I mean you'll give your usual helping hand! Now, where do we go from here?

S: (Creeping on, carrying a gadget which he uses to scan the room and some of the children.) All clear for bugging devices. Whoever the mole is, they aren't listening in on us.

Z: (Creeping on, she moves up to M and speaks sycophantically.) So, great leader, in your great experience, what's our next move?

M: Good question Z. O, what's our next move?

O: We need to wait for E. Where is he?

E: (Struggling on, carrying far too much equipment.) Coming!

O: What did you bring all that stuff for?

E: Z told me to!

Z: (Under the angry gaze of O.) Er, no, I didn't! I just told him to bring what he thought we needed…

O: E, put some of that stuff down. We don't need it.

E drops everything on the floor (safely) and salutes O.

E: Yes, ma'am!

O: M, you go alone down the right, S and Z, you go left and E and I'll follow up. I want to keep my eye on you, E.

M: OK, team, on my mark, as quietly as you can. Remember we need the element of surprise. (Pause.) Let's go!

M charges down the right of the hall shouting as loudly as he can and hides behind a handily placed leader a few feet from the stage. O buries her head in her hands. S and Z proceed stealthily down the other side of the hall, taking it in turns to move ahead a short distance, then hiding behind a child or leader. O and E move through the children down the middle of the hall, dodging from behind one child to another. E should introduce himself to each child he hides behind, making small talk with them, maybe asking them about their favourite football teams. E should get chatting to one child and get left behind by O. She then has to radio him.

O: (Into walkie-talkie.) O to E, O to E… come on! (E doesn't respond, but carries on chatting.) O to E, O to E. Stop talking and hurry up!

E doesn't answer and O has to go back to him.

O: (Pulling E by the arm away from his conversation.) Come on, E!

E: I was only having a quick chat!

O: This is a secret mission, not a cocktail party! Hurry up!

E: Sorry… you don't think I'm the mole, do you?

O: No, I don't think the mole would be as stupid as you.

E: (Smiling.) Oh thanks, that's really kind. (He realises what she means.) Hang on, hey!

O: Come on! (Into walkie-talkie.) O to M, O to M. Come in, M.

We hear loud snores. M has fallen asleep again. O puts her head in her hands.

O: E, go and wake M up! (E goes over to M and starts poking him in the shoulder.)

S: (Into walkie-talkie.) S to O, we're outside the station. Request further instructions.

O: (Into walkie-talkie.) O to S. Hold your position. We are having trouble with M.

S: Fallen asleep again?

O: Correct.

Z: (To S.) What's going on?

S: M has fallen asleep again.

Z: (To herself, laughing evilly.) What a stupid fool! I'm surprised he hasn't been fired!

S: What did you say?

Z: Er, um… I said he must be very tired.

E: M, wake up, we're all outside the station!

M: (Waking up.) What? Eh? The station? Have we caught them? Good-o, let's go home. Then I can write the report to say how I bravely captured the enemy agents single-handedly, sorted out world poverty and invented a new recipe for chicken tikka masala!

E: No, M, we've not even entered the station yet.

M: Oh right. Well, come on. What are we waiting for? (Into walkie-talkie.) M to O. What's the hold-up? Let's get going!

O: (Into walkie-talkie.) OK, agents, after three, everyone enter the station. S and Z, you go in through the fire exit, M through the side entrance and E and I'll go through the ticket office. Three!

The team make their way onto the stage from three different directions. M moves ostentatiously, with exaggerated spy movements, S scans everything he sees with his scanner, O moves like the experienced spy she is, Z doesn't bother with stealth, as she knows there are no enemy agents to catch. She could laugh quietly at the antics of the others. E manages to fall over various things (leaders, whatever set you have for your 'station'). O crouches down centre stage to examine something on the floor. M, who hasn't noticed

her crouch down, sees her and mistakes her for an enemy agent. He picks up a large piece of cloth (hanging as if it is curtain), gestures to E and they both creep up on O, throwing the cloth over her and shouting triumphantly.

M: Gotcha! O! O! I've caught them! We've got the enemy agents!

O struggles inside the cloth, but is still held down by M. The others look around for O. Z looks on in amusement.

E: O! Where are you?

O lets out a muffled shout from underneath the cloth.

E: What was that?!

S: (Scanning O.) M, I don't think this is an enemy agent…

O: (From underneath the cloth.) Get off me, you idiot!

M: O? Is that you?

O: (Struggling out from underneath the cloth.) Yes, of course it's me. Who did you think? Cheryl Cole?

S: (Scanning all around.) My scanner isn't reading anyone in here except us.

E: Do you mean we've missed them?

O: I don't think there were any enemy agents here. Either our intelligence was wrong, or the mole has struck again. How can we ever complete this message?

S: Incoming message!

Z: (Looking up in the air.) It's that pigeon again. I'll get you, you pesky bird!

Z is pooed on again (either pretend, or using the same method used for episode 2). E picks up a message from behind a piece of set.

E: But it dropped the message again. It's from the Chief! It says, 'Don't

despair, I know things are tough. But you will succeed in your mission, agents!'

O: Well, I'm glad he has confidence in us! Perhaps we will succeed.

M, O, S and E leave the stage.

Z: Well, I may have got pooed on, but at least those stupid agents are no nearer to rescuing the papers. (She laughs and exits, to the boos of the children.)

Mission 4
Capturing the mole

PROPS
- Torn paper
- Heroic music
- Rope
- Scroll

The scene is the safe house from episode 2, but all the screens and gadgets have gone, stolen by enemy agents. The sections torn by Z from the messages during episode 2 should be on the floor. The agents enter looking downcast.

M: Well, maybe that episode won't make it into my autobiography, 'Agent M – Star of the Secret Service'.

Z: (Laughing to herself.) What a big-headed fella…

M: What?

Z: Er, um… I said that will be a best-seller!

M: Yes, it will. (Heroic music starts, the others look at each other in dismay.) It tells the stories of my great triumphs! Rescuing the Princess of Germanland from the Evil King, seizing the secrets of the Mines of Goldonia from the enemy, inventing the television, introducing potatoes to the people of Britain, marrying Davina McCall…

O: You didn't do any of those things!

S: Hang on a minute! Where's all the equipment?

O: It was here when we left – it must have been stolen! The mole! Right! (Turning on M, E and S.) Which one of you is it? 'The mole is male'. That's what the message from HQ said. So, come on! Own up!

M, E and S protest their innocence all at once.

O: Well, M. You keep falling asleep – you've done nothing to help solve the case, but you seem certain that you'll get all the glory. S, you decoded the message from Agent G – how would we know if you changed some of the details? And E… well, E, you're just a useless agent!

O, M and E start arguing about who the mole is and who it isn't. Z stands watching them, smiling. E wanders dejectedly away from the group, sad that he has been called useless. Suddenly he spots the torn bits of paper on the floor and picks them up. He reads them and then realises what they are. He rushes to O.

E: O! O! Look what I've found!

O: (Sarcastically.) Oh, I can't imagine. Another half-eaten sandwich? (She looks at the bits of paper E is showing her.) Bits of paper? Oh, come on, E. These are just bits of paper a mouse has chewed.

E: Well, I thought they might have meant someth—

O: (Suddenly realising what the bits of paper are.) Paper a mouse has chewed! Let me see them!

E gives her the bits of paper.

O: These are blank, but this one says 'fe' and this one says 'petrol'. S, have you still got the messages? Give them to me!

S: (Handing her the messages.) Here they are.

O starts to fit the bits of paper into the messages with S and E looking on. Z looks uncertain about what's going to happen. M just looks mystified!

O: That's it! The messages read, 'Enemy agents are hiding at the petrol station.' and, 'Beware! There is a mole. Identity unknown. Mole is female.'

M, S and E look suspiciously at O. Meanwhile Z is looking desperately for a way out.

O: Not me, you idiots, her!

Z: Busted!

M: Get her!

A brief chase ensues, where M and E crash into each other and S gets pushed to the ground. Finally, O manages to catch Z.

S: Got her!

M: I knew it was her all along.

O: Well, why didn't you say?

M: What? Erm, um… I wanted to help you discover it for yourselves. Yes, a training activity, that's it.

O: (Fed up with M's boastfulness.) Shut. Up.

E: What shall we do with her?

O: We should take her to Spy HQ, but we still might have time to catch the enemy agents at the petrol station! It's not quite 13.00 hours yet. They'll still be there! Let's just tie her up here. E, I suppose you can tie her up; you do remember that from Spy School, don't you?

E: Of course! Top of the class, I was!

O: Good. E, you tie her up. S, you go and find whatever equipment that wasn't stolen. Meet M and me outside in one minute.

M, S and O rush off. E picks up a rope and tries to tie Z up.

E: (Fiddling with the rope.) Now, through this loop, round that end, double back, push it through and you're done! Well, I think that's how you do it. I only came top of rope class by copying Agent J. It'll do. (Shouting in the direction of the exit.) Wait for me, guys!

E runs off, leaving Z alone on stage.

Z: Well, they may have caught me, but it's not over yet. (She wriggles out of the ropes easily.) That E – what an idiot! Have you noticed?

He's got slip-on shoes! Can't even tie his own shoelaces! They'll not get far, and even if they do manage to rescue the Operation Moses Rescue papers, I'll be waiting for them! (**She leaves, laughing.**)

Pause, then shouting can be heard offstage, as the agents recount their battle to recapture the papers. The agents enter while saying this dialogue, with O carrying a scroll – the Operation Moses Rescue papers.

S: Did you see when I disabled their alarm system with a semi-repeating binary continuum, linked to their infinity loop with a random 341 pattern?

E: Er, what?

M: I was majestic. Never has a rescue been performed with such style and finesse!

O: Well, you were quite good this time. And you didn't fall asleep. Well, team, we've completed the mission! I didn't think we'd do it, but everything came good in the end. We rescued the papers and captured a mole at the same time! I think we can all be proud of ourselves, we did a grea—

They suddenly stop short at the rope on the floor. They realise Z has escaped.

M: E, I thought you were meant to tie her up!

E: I did! She can't have escaped!

S: Well, she did.

O: Come on, we can't stay here – the enemy know all about this place. We need to get the papers back to Spy HQ. Let's go!

They all rush off stage.

Mission 5
The final escape

PROPS
- Empty boxes
- Screwed up newspaper
- Stage lighting
- Big red button
- Scroll
- Piece of paper

The scene is a mysterious building; you could dress the stage with empty boxes and screwed up newspaper. The team have managed to get lost, and they don't know which way to go. During this episode, a section of the stage needs to light up like a protected area that uses laser beams to stop anyone progressing further (this idea is used in many spy programmes and films). You could use green lights, or you could screen the upstage centre part of the stage off, and do this part of the episode out of sight of the children (who can use their imaginations!). Either way you do this, there needs to be a big red button for E to lean on by accident.

The team stumble onto stage, arguing. E is carrying the Operation Moses Rescue papers.

M: Well, I have my own inner compass, so I never get lost. It can't be my fault.

O: Shut up, M, that isn't helping.

E: We could have asked someone, you know!

O: We're meant to be secret agents! We can't just stop someone in the street and ask for directions!

S: Well, my infra-red navigation locator definitely says Spy HQ is in this direction.

E: What, through this warehouse?

O: S, are you sure you've put the right coordinates in?

M: We could have used my SatNav, you know!

O: No way – it's got your voice on it. I'm not having you telling me to (**She does an impression of his voice.**) 'Turn left here.' or 'Perform a U-turn at the next safe opportunity.'

E: Wait a minute, what's that over there? Shouldn't we just go that way and see where we end up?

E walks over towards the 'laser-protected' area. He turns back to face the others, level with the red button on the wall.

E: I mean, what's the worst that could happen?

As he says this, he leans on the big red button and the corridor lights up!

S: E! Get away from there! You've just turned on a neutron high combustibility nuclear laser Stun-o-ray defence system!

E: I did what?

S: You activated a defence system that will knock you unconscious if you walk into it!

O: Wait, what's that noise?

M: Sorry, that's my stomach; it's been a long time since breakfast.

O: No, not that. I think I can hear footsteps.

S scans the door through which they came in.

S: There are agents approaching. I think it's Z and she's not alone!

M: We're trapped! Oh, Mummy!

E: O, do something!

O: What can I do?

S: (**Looking at scanner.**) Incoming message! It's the pigeon again!

E: I'll get it! Here pidgie, pidgie!

E gets pooed on, either pretending, or using the method you used in

previous episodes. O picks up the message from a pile of newspaper.

O: It dropped the message. (**She opens it.**) It's how to disable the lasers! S, do you understand the instructions?

S: Yes, of course, it'll take me a couple of minutes.

O: Be quick!

M: (**Whimpering.**) Hurry up!

S fiddles with the big red button, looking at the instructions. Footsteps and shouts are heard offstage.

E: They're coming!

O: Come on, S!

S: I've almost done it! But it will only last a few seconds; we need to run as fast as possible! (**One last adjustment to the red button.**) There, done it!

The 'lasers' go out and the team run through the protected area, shouting 'Quick!' 'Hurry up!' E drops the Operation Moses Rescue papers on the way across and only realises when he has got to the other side.

E: I dropped the papers, I have to go back!

He rushes back to get them, with others shouting at him not to/to hurry up. As soon as E gets back across, Z and a couple of henchmen run on stage.

Z: Ah-ha! Got you now! There's no escape! You thought you'd outrun Z – the greatest evil agent of all time? You stupid people! Now, give me back the papers, and prepare to meet your doom!

M: Oh, Mummy!

O: You'll never get away with this, Z!

Z: Well, if you won't give them back to me, then I'll come and get them from you!

Z and the henchmen start to run across the laser area, but halfway across the laser comes back on and they are knocked unconscious. (If your laser area is out of sight, the team will need to react and let the children know what has happened.)

S: They've been knocked unconscious! We need to get them out of there!

M: But how?

S: I don't know. The controls are on the other side.

E: What happens if I flick this switch on the floor?

S: Not now, E. This is important.

E: I was just saying that there's this switch on the floor.

M: Quiet, E. This is agent talk!

E: Well, I was only saying…

O: Hang on; does anyone know why E can't flick that switch?

M, S: No.

E flicks the switch and the lasers go off.

O: Brilliant, E! Quick, let's get them to safety and back to Spy HQ!

The team gets Z and the henchmen out of the laser area.

E: But how will we find HQ – we're lost, remember?

The Chief suddenly appears onstage.

Chief: You're at Spy HQ! S, your instruments aren't broken. We have to disguise HQ; you can't have a big sign on the street saying, 'Spies in here!' Well done, team, for recovering the Operation Moses Rescue papers. Now we can carry on learning about God's rescue all those years ago, just as the children have been learning about it all this week. And well done in catching the mole! We've been looking for her for

some time. When she comes round, we've got some questions for her and her friends! Come on, agents, let's go and celebrate a mission completed!

They all leave, helping Z and the henchmen off too.

FILE 5

Mission possible!

Planning your session

When you come to plan each day, make sure you have read the descriptions of the programme in File 1. Select the activities according to the children you are likely to have at the club.

You do not need to include all the activities listed here in your programme.

MAKING YOUR CHOICE

There are many factors which will influence your choice of activities:

THE CHILDREN INVOLVED

The children should be the most important consideration when choosing the daily activities. Children respond differently to the same activity. Spymasters in particular should bear this in mind when planning Going undercover.

THE LENGTH OF THE CLUB

Simply, if you have a long club, then you will be able to do more! The timings given are merely guidelines; different children will take different lengths of time to complete the same activity. Be flexible in your timings, judge whether it would be more valuable to complete an activity, even though it may be overrunning, rather than cut it short and go on to the next activity. Have something in your programme you can drop if things overrun.

THE LEADERS AVAILABLE

Not every club will be able to find leaders with the necessary skills to fulfil every requirement. If you can't find anyone with a Basic Food Hygiene Certificate, you will have to limit the refreshments you can provide. If you don't have musicians, then you'll have to rely on backing tracks or miss out the singing.

To help Spymasters prepare for Going undercover, the questions for each day are called Bible discovery notes and can be found in each mission and on the website.

MISSION START

SUNDAY SERVICE 1

God's mission

KEY PASSAGE
Exodus 1

KEY AIMS
- to see that God's people were in trouble but to discover that God had a rescue plan
- to kick off MISSION:RESCUE!

KEY STORY
We discover the trouble God's people were in, but look forward to God's rescue mission swinging into action!

This service introduces the club, but is not part of the club programme. It is possible to miss this out and not lose anything from the programme. However, this is a fantastic chance to get children and their families, especially those with little or no church background, to come into church and be welcomed. It will also help to engage them in the life of the church. Think carefully about how you can use this service to enable the most number of children and their families to attend.

For children with no church background
This may be one of the first times that children and their families beyond the reach of the church have been to a service, so make sure they are welcomed warmly (but not put off by too much attention). They will probably have no idea about any of the names mentioned in the Bible story today, so make sure your communication is clear and doesn't use any church jargon. They will be familiar with situations where they feel trapped and unhappy, and you can use this as a way into the story of the Israelites in Egypt (but don't dwell on their unhappiness.)

For church children
Church children will have probably heard of the story of Joseph and of Moses, but may not have put them together and will probably not have heard this part of the narrative. Help church children (and their families) piece together these stories and encourage them to think about how God wanted to rescue his people, and also how he wants to rescue us too.

For children from other faiths
Helping children from other faiths feel welcome and safe will be vital in the first session. Simple things like reassuring them that food will be suitable for them and making it clear what the club is about will be important. Do try really hard to pronounce their names correctly. If you're not sure how to pronounce them, ask.

For children with additional needs
Starting something new will feel like a potential threat to a child with an autistic spectrum disorder (ASD) or attention deficit hyperactive disorder (ADHD).

A clear schedule of activities will give confidence and encourage calm behaviour. It's all about relationships. Make sure each child knows who will help them and where they can go if they need time out (maybe a beanbag in a corner.)

In today's story God's people needed help. God has a plan to help each of us and you can be showing children what that is like, by the way you work alongside them

PRACTICAL PREPARATIONS

☐ **Registration** Registration forms, badges, labels, pens, team lists

☐ **Music** The CodeCrackers band or backing tracks

☐ **Drama** Costume and props

☐ **Q-Tech** PA system, laptop, PowerPoints and projection/OHP and acetates, MISSION:RESCUE DVD

☐ **Agents X and Y** Running order, notes, a variety of boxes for Operation: build (ask for the church's help in collecting these in advance)

☐ **The mad laboratory** A range of refreshments for after the service

☐ **Spy Chief** Story script, bag/box of Lego® bricks

On the mission

OPENING AND WELCOME

The church leader should play the part of the head of the Secret Service, 'N', and should welcome everyone to the first session of MISSION:RESCUE accordingly! Introduce the idea of spies, and that all the children in the club are Agents, who will discover all about God's mission – to rescue his people. Introduce Agents X and Y, who will lead the children through the different sessions of MISSION:RESCUE. N explains to Agents X and Y that God has a mission and the Agents have to find out all about it. All the details are to be found in God's book (the Bible), in the section called Exodus. N tells X and Y to help the children to crack the codes, read the messages and discover all about God's mission to rescue his people! N then leaves X and Y to lead the next part of the service.

MISSION:RESCUE SONG AND WORSHIP

X and Y should introduce the CodeCrackers and get them to teach the children the MISSION:RESCUE song. Once you have sung that through a couple of times, sing some other songs of worship to God. Select ones that your church are familiar with that talk about God's power and God's faithfulness. Remember that you may have people unused to church in your service, so try to avoid any songs with lyrics that will be confusing or that mean they will be singing something that they don't necessarily believe.

PRAYER

Lead everyone in a prayer (making sure you explain what you're doing) thanking God for bringing everyone here today, and asking him to help you have a good time and learn more about his rescue mission.

HEARING THE MESSAGE

Invite a member of the congregation to read Exodus 1. Ask someone who can read the story well, with plenty of expression. This may be the first time some people will hear the Bible and it should be an exciting encounter! Use a child-friendly version of the Bible, such as the Contemporary English Version.

OPERATION: BUILD

Explain that every day at MISSION:RESCUE, some of the Agents will undergo a challenge to test their spy potential. Today's challenge is building the tallest tower out of the boxes provided. (Depending on how many boxes you have collected, the volunteers can do this in turn or at the same time, with the same number of boxes each.) Get some volunteers and see who can build the tallest tower! Congratulate the winner (and have a small prize if appropriate).

SPY CHIEF'S CLUES

X and Y introduce the Spy Chief and ask him what his clues are for today. The Chief should bring a large bag/box full of Lego®. X and Y should wonder what this clue means, and ask the congregation for ideas. Y should come up with some silly ideas, and X introduces the Agents to the question she will ask Y throughout the club: 'But why, Y?' She should encourage the Agents to say it with her. When they finally have to admit that they don't know, the Chief goes on to tell his story, using his clue, in his own words or following this script:

REVEALING THE SECRET

Does anyone know the story of Joseph, the one with the coloured coat? (Get some details from the congregation.) Joseph went to Egypt and ended up helping Pharaoh, the Egyptian king, out! Then he brought his whole family to live with him in Egypt. Our story begins years after Joseph died. But Joseph's family were still in Egypt. There were lots of them, so many of them, in fact, that the Egyptians were scared of them. The pharaoh that Joseph helped had died and a new king had come to power who didn't know anything of the things Joseph had done. He only saw the number of Israelites – that's what Joseph's family were called – and wanted to stop them growing. He was scared that they might take control of his country.

So he tried to wear them down with hard work. (Start to build things with the Lego®, and invite some children to help you build. Carry on with the story as they build.) He forced them to build huge cities where he could store all his supplies. But even though they worked very hard and were badly treated by the

FILE 5

Egyptians, the number of Israelites still got bigger! Can you imagine that? And the Egyptians and their king hated them even more. So they made the Israelites work so hard that their lives were miserable! (Check on how the building is going. Comment on how good they are, but how much harder the Israelites had to work.) But the Israelites still grew in number. (Pour out all the Lego® bricks left in the box and spread them out on the floor, so that as many of the congregation can see as possible.) You may think that there are a lot of Lego® bricks here, but there were even more Israelites. The book of Exodus in the Bible tells us that there were over six hundred thousand of them! Can you imagine that?

The pharaoh was so scared that he decided to do something drastic and terrible. He decided that he would make an order that every Israelite boy born was to be killed straight away. He was very scared and hated the Israelites so much that he was willing to kill some of them! However, even though Pharaoh was a powerful and scary man, the women who helped the babies to be born didn't do what they were told, and let all the babies live. They were faithful to God.

Eventually the pharaoh got so angry and scared that he told his soldiers to throw the baby boys into the river! Can you imagine that? The lives of the Israelites were still terrible, but God hadn't forgotten them. He had a plan to save them and it involved a lot of things that are hard to imagine: a baby in a basket; a bush that was on fire but didn't burn; a stick that turns into a snake; frogs, flies and lots of other crawly things, and a sea that opened up to let people walk through! And at MISSION:RESCUE, we're going to hear about this rescue plan, a man called Moses and the powerful God who put it all into action and rescued his people!

SONG
Sing the MISSION:RESCUE song together as it will remind everyone of some of the details of the story you are going to hear during the club.

CHECKING THE EVIDENCE
If you have time, include a quiz here on today's story. Make sure you include the whole congregation – children, young people and adults. Introduce the spy gadget that will score the quiz for the whole week (see page 10).

TODAY'S MISSION
After the quiz, X and Y should review the day's story, talking through these points:
- The Israelites' lives had got worse and worse. They were respected when Joseph was alive, but that was soon forgotten and they were badly treated.
- The pharaoh hated the Israelites and tried to destroy them by working them hard and getting rid of some of the baby boys.
- But God was still with the Israelites, protecting them. He had a rescue mission in mind, and he was going to save his people from slavery. And this is what we're going to discover at MISSION:RESCUE!

SPY SONGS
Sing a couple of songs here that fit with the theme of God having a plan and God rescuing. Remember to keep the lyrics simple and jargon-free! For ideas on which songs to use, take a look at the list on the MISSION: RESCUE website.

THE GODCODE
Unlike spies, we don't need to keep any secrets from God – we can be open and honest with him. Before the session, create a spy prayer action that you can do just before you pray (see the MISSION:RESCUE website for examples). You might also want to invent a spy shout (or whisper!) of 'Amen' when you finish praying. Teach the congregation the action (and shout, if you're using one) and then say a simple prayer thanking God for being ready to rescue his people. Thank God also for MISSION:RESCUE and ask him to keep you safe and help you have fun as you learn more about him.

SPY SONGS
Sing the MISSION:RESCUE song again to finish the service. Make sure all the children know about the first session of the club and have registration forms on hand so that children can sign up. Give out any information about family events that you're running alongside the club, and about any other appropriate events in your church's programme.

AFTER THE SERVICE
After the service has finished, make sure all new children and families are welcomed. It might be an idea to have some kind of family event, maybe involving food. What you can do is dictated by the skills you have on the team, your facilities and the situation you're running your club in, but see if there's anything that will fit all these considerations.

MISSION 1
Undercover

Mission briefing

SPIRITUAL PREPARATION

READ TOGETHER
Read Exodus 2 together. (Think creatively about how you read such a large section of text, bearing in mind the attention span of junior leaders!)

EXPLORE TOGETHER
Split the team into three roughly equal groups and ask one group to look at verses 1 to 10, another to look at verses 11 to 15 and the third to look at verses 15b to 25. Ask each group to consider these questions:
- What rescue is taking place?
- Who is doing the rescuing and why?
- What part does this story play in God's wider rescue mission for his people?

When all the groups have finished, gather back together and feed back the thoughts of each group.

REFLECT TOGETHER
Out of such a terrible situation – the new pharaoh ordering the death of all Israelite newborn boys – God starts working for the release of his people. Moses is saved by people who love him: mainly his mother and sister. But he's also saved by an unlikely source – the king's daughter. Later, Moses attempts to take the rescue mission into his own hands when he kills an Egyptian slave master to save one of his people. As is often the case when we try to move God's plans forward under our own steam, Moses comes unstuck and has to flee to Midian. Finally in this chapter, Moses is rescued by Jethro, who provides Moses with a secure life and family.

KEY PASSAGE
Exodus 2:1–10 (and 11–25 for 8 to 11s)

KEY AIMS
- to discover that God has a plan to rescue his people
- to start to understand that God protects us
- to welcome the children, start building relationships and have fun together

KEY STORY
God rescues Moses, preparing him for the rescue mission.

For children with no church background
This story is unusual and contains many details that will interest children who have never heard it before. They will undoubtedly have questions about Moses' basket or why the princess was having a bath in the river. Answer these questions, but make sure you point the children back to what God is doing in this story – he wants to rescue his people and Moses is a big part of that mission. God protects Moses so that he can play his part!

For church children
Church children will probably have heard this story before – it is the subject of many children's Bible story books. However, they may not have placed the story in the wider narrative of God rescuing his people. Encourage the children to enjoy the story again, but start to help them think about what God is doing and why. Throughout the club, keep returning to the idea of God's rescue plan – where does the day's story fit?

For children from other faiths
Moses is a prophet in Islam and so if you have any Muslim children they will have heard of Moses, but they might not know this story. In Islam he's called Musa so they might use this name for him. They may think it's wrong to have pictures of prophets so you might want to explain why, as Christians, we think it's OK.

For children with additional needs
As you come to know the children more, you will be able to identify what extra resources you may need. Children with learning difficulties will understand more if objects are used; perhaps a cloth for the river and figures that they can move as they retell the story. Think about learning a few signs. Find them at **www.britishsignlanguage.com** or **www.deafchristian.org.uk**

Moses was kept safe by God. Encourage the children to say what makes them feel safe. As you understand their anxieties more, you will be able to connect better.

The day's aim is to discover that God has a plan to rescue and that he protects us. Reflect on how the day's story shows God's protection over his people. Spend some time thinking about how God has protected you. How has he rescued you?

PRAY TOGETHER

- Pray for the children you know are coming today by name, and pray for those not yet registered who will turn up on the door.
- Pray for the events you have planned today.
- Pray for relationships to be formed, for a warm and welcoming atmosphere.
- Pray for each other, about any specific worries or needs that you have. Pray also that God will give you everything you need as you work for him.

PRACTICAL PREPARATION

Talk through your programme together, ensuring that everyone knows their part in the day and has everything they need. Set up the different areas of the club and make sure that everything is in place. Encourage the team to greet children who came to the first service (if you held one) and welcome those for whom this is the first day at the club.

WHAT YOU NEED CHECKLIST

- ☐ **Registration** Registration forms, badges, labels, pens, team lists
- ☐ **Spy Rings** Bibles, Secret Files or Spy Sheets, Bible discovery notes
- ☐ **Music** The CodeCrackers band or backing tracks
- ☐ **Drama** Costume and props
- ☐ **Q-Tech** PA system, laptop, PowerPoints and projection/OHP and acetates, MISSION:RESCUE DVD
- ☐ **Activities** Equipment for games and construction
- ☐ **Agents X and Y** Running order, notes, Spy Chief's clues, quiz questions, sleeping bag, Operation: disguise equipment
- ☐ **The mad laboratory** Drinks and biscuits, or other refreshments
- ☐ **Spy Chief** Props for the story; picture of a well and a river (see MISSION:RESCUE website); story script

On the mission

As the children arrive and register, play some spy-themed music (such as Bond or Mission Impossible theme tunes) and display the MISSION:RESCUE logo on the screen to welcome the children.

As this is the first main day of the club, make sure the registration team are ready to greet and register the children, so that any new children and parents don't have to wait long. Have a welcome team on hand to take the Agents to their Spy Ring. Encourage Spymasters and Assistants to be ready to welcome the children in their groups, tell them where the toilets are etc.

AGENTS' BRIEFING

10 minutes

Choose one of these activities to do as the children arrive. The spy base activity could be a week long activity, depending on how ambitious you are. The secret identity activity is particularly suitable if you don't have much space.

SPY BASE
What you need
- ☐ Sheets, blankets, large cardboard boxes etc
- ☐ Sticky or parcel tape
- ☐ Poles, posts, chairs, even clothes horses!

What you do
Before the session, gather together some materials that you can use to create a spy base for each Spy Ring. As the Agents arrive, Spymasters should challenge their Spy Ring to build a spy base where they can meet and discuss their spy secrets without other Spy Rings hearing! For child protection purposes, try to make the base open at the front, so that everything is open and accountable. As you work, chat with the children so that you can get to know them at the start of the club. You could come up with your own password or Spy Ring phrase (this could be used as a call and response, to rally your Spy Ring). Agents X and Y should go round the bases, to see how the Spy Rings are getting on.

SECRET IDENTITIES
What you need
- ☐ Disguises, such as glasses, false facial hair, hats etc
- ☐ Sticky labels
- ☐ Felt-tip pens

What you do
As the Agents arrive, ask them to make up a spy name to go alongside their real name. Encourage them to

write their spy names on the labels, then to decorate them. When they have done that, have fun disguising each other with the hats, glasses etc. As you work, chat with the children so that you can get to know them at the start of the club.

ACTIVE AGENTS

45 minutes

Bring everyone together so that the Agents can get active! Play the MISSION:RESCUE theme song as a sign for the children to join the larger group.

Agents X and Y should introduce themselves and welcome everyone to MISSION:RESCUE. They should run through the day's programme briefly and tell everyone where the toilets are and what to do in the event of a fire. Set out any simple rules that you have for the club. X and Y should spot the screen for the Operation disguise game and wonder with the children what it could be for. Introduce the dead letter drop, where Agents can leave secret messages – well, jokes, pictures and questions for Agents X and Y!

Agent Y should now reveal his sleeping bag and ask Agent X why she hasn't brought one. Then Y should get in his sleeping bag, explaining to X (who he thinks is obviously stupid) that it is essential for today's theme. X should confide in the children that she doesn't think Y is a very good spy. Introduce a shout that can be used throughout the club: 'But why, Y?!' and get the children to shout it out now.

Y should reveal that he is going undercover, and that X should at least have a duvet or a blanket. X should realise the mistake Y has made, and explain what 'going undercover' actually means, getting help from the Agents as she explains Y's mistake. X should then explain the theme of the day – being undercover! Leave the sleeping bag somewhere out of the way on the stage – it will stay there during the club as a reminder of this first day.

SPY WORKOUT

The Spy Fitness Instructor (SFI) should introduce the workout, telling the Agents that they have to be fit to carry out their rescue mission! Go through a short programme of simple exercises while playing spy music in the background. If you have any children with special needs, make sure you include actions that they feel comfortable doing.

SPY SONGS

Introduce the CodeCrackers and get them to teach the children the MISSION:RESCUE theme song, together

with the actions. For this first day, practise it a couple of times, so that the Agents get the hang of it, rather than singing other songs at this point. Say that you'll sing it again later!

OPERATION: DISGUISE

Introduce today's special operation. Challenge the Spy Rings to spot the five different members of the Secret Service in disguise! Each Secret Service Member will pop their heads above a screen twice in different disguises. Agents should tell their Spymaster who they think it is, and the Spymaster should write the name down. Before the session, gather together wigs, hats, glasses, false moustaches and beards – anything that could be used as a facial disguise. Ask your five SSMs to put together two disguises from what you have provided, and agree an order in which they will appear in their different disguises. (Make sure they can all change easily from their first to their second disguise – this may need some practice!)

At the start of the game, get all of the SSMs to pop their heads above the screen and tell the children their names (you could put their names on the screen, so that the children have a reminder). Then, when the first disguises are ready, the SSMs should pop their heads above the screen in turn. Keep this moving quickly so that it is fun, but not too difficult. When the game is finished, go through the answers and congratulate everyone on their surveillance skills!

SECURITY REPORT

Introduce the Head of Security (maybe wearing a T-shirt of the security level colour), who will give their report for the day:

- Security level aquamarine.
- Y now understands the idea behind 'going undercover'. He has a sleeping bag for sale, if anyone wants to buy it.
- The Israelites are in a terrible position – they need someone to hear their cries and save them!
- God is setting out to rescue his people!
- Repeat: security level aquamarine! Stay alert, Agents!

SPY CHIEF'S CLUES

Introduce the Spy Chief and ask him to reveal his clues for today. The Spy Chief should have a baby doll, basket (if you can get hold of a Moses basket, even better!), a picture of a river, some long grasses (these could be long, thin, green pieces of paper), a crown, a club or big stick, a picture of a well and a toy sheep. Make sure the children know what all the objects are and ask them what they might mean. Get some suggestions from the Agents, and Agent Y should make some stupid suggestions (such as the basket being a boat for a royal sheep or the long grasses being a hula skirt). X and the children should shout, 'But why, Y?!' after each daft suggestion. After a few minutes, ask the Spy Chief to explain a bit more about what these clues mean.

REVEALING THE SECRET

The Spy Chief should thank X and Y and go on to tell the story using the clues, or introduce today's episode from the MISSION:RESCUE DVD. (If you are telling the story and using the DVD, tell the story with the clues first, then show the DVD.) The Spy Chief should tell the story in their own words or use this script:

Long ago, God's people, that's the people who loved God and followed his way (they were called the Israelites), were in trouble. They were living in Egypt, but the people of Egypt were scared of them! The king – he was called the pharaoh – was scared too, and he made them into slaves. That meant they had to do everything the pharaoh said; they had no choice. But God had not forgotten about his people. He wanted to rescue them and lead them into a new country, where they would be free to follow God's way and not be slaves. But first God had to rescue one person, and it was a very dangerous mission!

The pharaoh wanted to get rid of all the Hebrew baby boys, but the mother of one Hebrew baby boy wanted to save her son. (Show the doll.) So she got a basket (Show the basket.) and painted it with tar to make it waterproof. Then she put her baby in the basket and put it in the river! (Put the doll in the basket, then show the picture of the river.) But, because she had made it waterproof, it didn't sink, but floated off down the river. The baby's sister, called Miriam, went undercover and watched the basket to see what would happen.

The basket didn't float off too far, but got stuck in some tall grass next to the river. (Show the long grasses.) And who was having a bath in the river (yes, in the river, that seems strange, doesn't it?) but the pharaoh's daughter. (Show the crown.) She saw the basket in the long grass and sent one of her servant girls to get it out of the river. When she opened the basket, what did she find? A baby boy! (Take the doll out of the basket.) She realised it was a Hebrew baby, but instead of telling her dad so he could get rid of it, she decided to keep the baby.

Miriam saw what had happened and went up to the princess. 'Shall I find someone to look after the baby for you?' she asked. The princess thought for a moment

and then agreed. So Miriam went off to get her (and the baby's) mum. So, the baby's mum looked after him for the princess. Then, when the baby was old enough, he went to live in the palace. And the pharaoh's daughter called him Moses. God had rescued Moses, because he wanted Moses to play a big part in his rescue mission!

But Moses wasn't out of danger for long! For one of God's agents, he certainly knew how to get into trouble. One day, Moses saw an Egyptian hitting one of the Hebrews. (Show the club or large stick.) Moses saw that no one else was around, so he killed the Egyptian. (Swing the club as if hitting someone.) He tried to rescue the Hebrew, but he wasn't following God's plan! Before long, everyone had heard about what Moses had done, even the pharaoh, and Moses ran for his life!

He ran and ran till he got to a land called Midian, where he sat down next to a well. (Show the picture of the well.) He must have thought everything had gone wrong – he was so far from home, and he couldn't go back, because he had done something really bad. But God didn't leave him sitting there. Some girls, daughters of a man called Jethro, came along. They were looking after some of their father's sheep. (Show the toy sheep.) Moses helped them and they took him to Jethro. Jethro was a friend of God, and he looked after Moses. God had rescued him again. But was Moses ready to find out his part in God's rescue mission? We'll find out tomorrow!

CHECKING THE EVIDENCE

X and Y should thank the Spy Chief, then introduce the quiz. Before the session, put together some questions about the story, and also include some that are about the other parts of the morning so far (eg the workout or Operation disguise). You could include:

- What did Y use to go undercover? (A sleeping bag.)
- Who was sent undercover in today's story? (Moses.)
- Who followed her brother to see what would happen? (Miriam.)
- When Moses grew up, what did he do wrong? (Killed an Egyptian.)

Make the quiz quick and lively, so the children have a chance to review the story and let off some steam after sitting and listening to the story. Introduce the point-awarding gadget and use it to award points (see page 10).

TODAY'S MISSION

After the quiz, X and Y should briefly review the day's story, talking through these points:

- God knew that his people were in trouble, and had a plan to rescue them.

- God rescued Moses three times (as a baby, escaping from the pharaoh after murdering someone and through Jethro taking him in), so that he could be part of the rescue mission.
- Moses had made a mess of things and was a long way from home, but God was still going to use him to rescue his people. God had protected Moses – he was a big part of the rescue plan.
- God has a plan for us too. And even if we feel like everything has gone wrong, God will always be with us and protect us. He will pick us up and set us back on the right road.

THE GODCODE

Tell the children that you are going to talk to God, but that you don't need any special codebreakers, signals or passwords to chat with him. We can be open and honest, because he hears us loud and clear and we don't need to have any secrets from him. Before the session, create a spy prayer action that you can do just before you pray (see the MISSION:RESCUE website for examples). You might also want to invent a spy shout (or whisper!) of 'Amen' when you finish praying. Teach the children the action (and shout if you're using one) and then say a simple prayer, thanking God for the club so far, thanking him for rescuing Moses and asking him to be with everyone as they go to their Spy Rings.

SPY SONGS

Sing the MISSION:RESCUE theme song again, together with one or two songs that reflect the theme of the day. You could choose:

- 'Twisting back in time' Light for Everyone (SU)
- 'Our God is a great big God' Songs of Fellowship (Kingsway Music)

After the songs, introduce the Interrogation section, where Agents will be able to question a member of the Secret Service. Encourage the Spy Rings to think of questions to ask that SSM. Then send everyone to their spy bases to explore the story more.

GOING UNDERCOVER

45 minutes

THE MAD LABORATORY
Dead letter drop

Serve your chosen refreshments, inventing funny names for them if you wish or have a kitchen laboratory as mentioned on page 10. Chat together about the club so far. What are the children's favourite parts? Remind the Ring to think of questions for today's interrogation and write them down for Agents

X and Y to ask later. Remind them also of the dead letter drop, where they can leave their jokes and pictures. Go on to explore the Bible passage together more closely.

BIBLE DISCOVERY
With older children

Remind the children of the situation God's people found themselves in. Challenge the children to retell the story of Moses being saved in the basket, using the pictures on page 5 of Secret Files. Go on to read Exodus 2:11–15 (from page 6 or a Bible) and decide what Moses did wrong. Say that Moses tried to do some rescuing of his own, but that he wasn't following God's plan. The children are likely to accept that Moses was wrong to kill the Egyptian. They often have a clear sense of justice and may question Moses escaping punishment by Pharaoh. If so, explain that there are consequences: he has to leave Egypt, his family and princely status, and run off to the desert for many years. If it comes up, think about times when we haven't followed God's way, but don't dwell for too long on this, as it will come up later. Solve the maze on page 7. Read Exodus 2:15b–22 (on page 8) and, if you have an appropriate story, share a time when you (or someone you know) were 'rescued' by God.

Look at page 9 and crack the code to find the secret words in the final part of Exodus 2. Chat for a while about how God heard the prayers of his people and hadn't forgotten that they were still in trouble. Comment on how Christians can be reassured by this. Whatever your situation is, you can be certain that God knows what you're going through and cares deeply for you.

Use page 10 to reflect together on what the children may have done wrong that they want to say sorry for. Give some time for them to fill in the space, then say a simple prayer, thanking God that he forgives us if we are sorry.

With younger children

Remind the children of the situation God's people found themselves in. Look at the pictures together on Spy Sheet 1. Read out Exodus 2:1–10 to the group and let the children decide which pictures are a part of the story and which aren't. Encourage them to tick the pictures that form part of the story. Put the children into pairs and get them to retell the story to each other, using the right pictures. Be ready to help them if they need it.

Chat with the children about how God rescued Moses and protected him. If you have an appropriate story about how God rescued and/or protected you, tell the children about it now.

Encourage the children to think about what they want to say to God in response to today's story and write or draw it in the space at the bottom of the Spy Sheet. Chat about what the children have drawn and pray together if that seems appropriate. If there is time, go on to retell simply the story of Exodus 2:11–25.

With all age groups

Adapt these questions to suit your group, sharing your own feelings, opinions and experiences as appropriate:
- How do you think Moses' family felt when they had to put Moses in a basket in the river?
- If you were Moses' brother or sister, would you have trusted God to protect Moses?
- In what ways would Moses' life in the palace be different from his life at home? (Encourage the children to use their imaginations!)
- Do you think Moses was sorry for killing the Egyptian?
- How do you think Moses felt when he had to leave his home?
- If God rescued and protected Moses, even though he messed up, what does that tell us about God and how he might rescue and protect us?

Q-TECH'S WORKSHOP

Choose a construction activity from Q-Tech's spy store (see page 27), deciding whether to do an individual or an all-together construction. For extra ideas, see Ultimate Craft (SU, 978 1 84427 364 5).

SPIES' TIME OUT

Help the Agents let off steam by choosing suitable games from Q-Tech's spy store (see page 27). See page 10 for more info about choosing the best games for your club. For extra games ideas, check out Ultimate Games (SU, 978 1 84427 365 2).

AGENTS ARE GO!

25 minutes

DEAD LETTER DROP

Welcome everyone back together by playing the MISSION:RESCUE theme song. If there are any secret messages in the dead letter drop, read one or two out now (or have some pre-prepared to give the children the idea). Otherwise remind the Agents to bring in jokes and pictures tomorrow.

SPY SONGS

The CodeCrackers lead a song you have already sung this session.

RETURN OF THE SPY CHIEF

Welcome back the Spy Chief, who goes on to round up what the Spy Rings have been exploring together. The Spy Chief should sum up these points, using the clues from earlier:
- Basket: God rescued Moses three times, because he was going to play a big part in God's plan to rescue his people.
- Club or big stick: Sometimes we try to make things happen on our own, and mess up, like Moses did.
- Sheep: But God is always there, protecting us, ready to rescue us again, just like he rescued Moses through Jethro and his sheep!

INTERROGATION

Introduce the Secret Service member who is to be interrogated. Before the session, go through with the SSM what you're going to talk about – how God has protected (and maybe rescued) the SSM – making sure that their story is appropriate. Interrogate the SSM, including some of the questions the children have thought of. When you have finished, thank the SSM for being willing to be interrogated!

DRAMA: WHO'S THE MOLE?

Introduce the drama: 'Who's the mole?' Explain what a mole is, through Y being confused about what the characters in the drama are looking for, thinking they are looking for a small, furry creature that lives in a hole. After X has cleared up Y's confusion, introduce today's episode, where the agents find out some secret papers have been stolen.

CRACKING THE CODE

With the help of the CodeCrackers, start to learn the Learn and remember verse for MISSION:RESCUE – Psalm 118:24 – by singing the Learn and remember verse song 'The day'. See the MISSION:RESCUE website for details. Enjoy clapping out a rhythm together to fit with the song! This song is available on the MISSION: RESCUE DVD, Bitesize Bible Songs 2 and can be downloaded from Scripture Union's online shop.

If you're not using the song, start to learn the verse by using the code on the MISSION:RESCUE website. Either put it up on the screen or give each Spy Ring a copy for them to do in their groups. Give the Spy Rings a few moments to crack the code, then go through verse 24 together.

COMPLETING THE MISSION

Round off Agents are go! by asking the children what they have enjoyed at MISSION:RESCUE today and then include those things in a short prayer of thanks, using your spy prayer action (and shout). Sing the MISSION: RESCUE theme song and send the Agents back to their Spy Rings to round off the day's session.

AGENTS' DEBRIEF

10 minutes

As you sit together for the final time today, chat about the highlights of the day. Finish any pages of Secret Files or sections of the Spy Sheets you have not done, or carry on with the construction or activity from Agents' briefing. Alternatively, pray together using this prayer activity:

CHAT WITH GOD

What you need

☐ Felt-tip pens

☐ Small pieces of paper

What you do

Remind the Agents that you've been learning about God protecting and rescuing. Ask them to draw a place or situation where they want God to protect them. It might be at school, when they're riding their bike or when they have to do something they don't like. When everyone has finished, ask them to look at their piece of paper while you say a prayer asking for God's protection in that place/situation. Encourage the Agents to take their pictures home and remember that God will protect them in that place.

As the children are picked up from their Spy Rings, make sure they are reminded of the next session, and that they take all of their belongings with them. Make sure too that they remember to bring in jokes, pictures and questions for the dead letter drop. Each Spymaster should know how each of the children in their group is getting home.

MISSION CLEAR-UP

30 minutes

After all the children have gone, clear-up from the day's events and set up for the next session. Meet together as a team to debrief. Use a feedback system that works best for you – there is an evaluation form on the MISSION:RESCUE website. Have a brief time of prayer where Spymasters and assistants can pray for their groups, and other team members can pray for their areas of responsibility. If you have the time and the facilities, you may wish to share a meal together.

SPY SHEET 1
Undercover

Look at these pictures. Some of them come from today's story and some don't! Can you tell which is which?

Read Exodus 2:1–10 together and put a tick next to the things that are in the story.

Use the items you have ticked to retell the story of Moses in the river to your fellow agents. Get your Spymaster to help you if you forget anything.

God protected and rescued Moses because he had a big part to play in God's mission to save his people. He was with Moses all the time, and made sure he was safe. God protects us and keeps us safe too. What do you want to say to God about that? Write or draw it here:

MISSION 2

Your mission, should you choose to accept it

Mission briefing

SPIRITUAL PREPARATION

READ TOGETHER
Read Exodus 3:1 – 4:17 together. (Again this is a long passage, so try to come up with a creative way of reading this large chunk.)

EXPLORE TOGETHER
Split the team into smaller groups (for example, pairs or threes). Ask half the groups to look at Exodus 3, and the other half to explore Exodus 4:1–17. Ask each group to consider these questions:
- How is God communicating in this passage? What do you think of that?
- What does God give Moses?
- If you were in Moses' place, what would you think?
- What part does this story play in God's wider rescue mission for his people?

When all the groups have finished, gather back together and feed back the thoughts of each group.

KEY PASSAGE
Exodus 3:1–15

KEY AIMS
- to realise that God speaks and listens, and will give us everything we need
- to continue to build relationships with the children, and to welcome those who are new to the club today

KEY STORY
God meets with Moses and gives him the mission to bring his people out of Egypt. He gives Moses everything he'll need to carry out the mission.

For children with no church background
All children will be familiar with communication through new media – mobile phones, email, voice calls over the Internet – whether these methods are open to them or not. They are commonplace and we can sometimes forget how amazing they are. However, encourage children with little or no church background to wonder at God's chosen method of communication in this story. God chooses to speak with his people in a variety of different ways – nothing is impossible for him!

For church children
Like the story for Day 1, church children may already be familiar with this story, but help them explore it further by investigating God's conversation with Moses. That Moses thinks he's not the right person for this job will resonate with many children, who, because of their age or circumstance, can sometimes feel like they are not up to tasks that are given them. Give them a chance to see how God gave Moses everything he needed, and think how God promises the same for us.

For children from other faiths
The symbol of fire is a key part of this story. Children of other faiths will understand and recognise similar symbolism from their own traditions, such as the festivals of Diwali (light) and Holi (water/fire) for Hindus and Sikhs.

For children with additional needs
Moses was worried about being able to communicate. If you have children who do not have use of their voices they will still communicate in different ways: eye pointing, gesture, pointing to pictures or symbols or by signing. You could use a 'talking button' so that a child could join in and 'have their say' (£4 from www.inclusive.co.uk) or you might let a child teach the whole group some simple sign language.

REFLECT TOGETHER

After all he has been through, God knows Moses is going to need some convincing about playing his part in God's rescue mission. So, God goes about using just the right methods to catch Moses' attention and show him what he needs to do.

God gives Moses both strong reassurance and practical demonstrations of his power. In Exodus 3, God explains the mission and tells Moses what to say to the Israelites in Egypt. God knows that Moses is unsure (Moses tells him clearly enough!) so reassures him by making it clear that he hears the groans of his people and intends to rescue them. Then in verses 14 and 15 God says the most reassuring thing of all: that he is 'I Am'. With Moses still expressing his doubts, Exodus 4 shows God giving practical examples of his power, providing Moses with signs for the Israelites and finally bringing his brother Aaron to be the spokesperson to Pharaoh.

As you come to your club now, reflect together on how God speaks to you. What does God being 'I Am' mean to you, both personally and as part of the MISSION: RESCUE team? How has God given you all you need in your walk with him and during the club?

PRAY TOGETHER

- Pray for the children you know are coming today by name, and pray for those not yet registered who will turn up at the door.
- Pray for the events you have planned today.
- Pray that God will communicate clearly to everyone at the club today.
- Pray for continuing relationships, that children will continue to feel at home at MISSION:RESCUE.
- Pray for each other, about any specific worries or needs that you have. Pray also that God will give you everything you need as you work for him.

PRACTICAL PREPARATION

Talk through your programme together, ensuring that everyone knows their part in the day and has everything they need. Set up the different areas of the club and make sure that everything is in place. Make sure you make any adjustments you agreed in your evaluation time after the previous session.

WHAT YOU NEED CHECKLIST

- ☐ **Registration** Registration forms, badges, labels, pens, team lists
- ☐ **Spy Rings** Bibles, Secret Files or Spy Sheets, Bible discovery notes, pens and pencils, hieroglyph sheets
- ☐ **Music** The CodeCrackers band or backing tracks
- ☐ **Drama** Costume and props
- ☐ **Q-Tech** PA system, laptop, PowerPoints and projection/OHP and acetates, MISSION:RESCUE DVD, two ringtone sound effects, fire film clip/ picture
- ☐ **Activities** Equipment for games and construction
- ☐ **Agents X and Y** Running order, notes, Spy Chief's clues, quiz questions, normal mobile phone, giant mobile phone, Operation: communication, programme list, bucket of polystyrene chippings
- ☐ **The mad laboratory** Drinks and biscuits, or other refreshments
- ☐ **Spy Chief** story script

On the mission

As the children arrive and register, play some spy-themed music (such as Bond or Mission:Impossible theme tunes) and display the MISSION:RESCUE logo on the screen to welcome the children.

Have plenty of team available in the registration area to welcome any new children, chat to parents and make sure everyone knows where they are going. Spymasters and Assistants should be ready in their bases to welcome and chat with their Agents.

AGENTS' BRIEFING

10 minutes

Choose one of these activities to do as the children arrive. If you started the spy base activity in the previous session, carry on working together to create your base. Otherwise try this activity.

HIEROGLYPH MESSAGES
What you need
- ☐ Hieroglyph messages from the resource bank (page 34)
- ☐ Pens or pencils

What you do
Working together, singly or in pairs, use the hieroglyph key to crack the messages. How difficult was it to reveal the secrets within? Once you have all finished, try to write some of your own messages for the other Agents in your Spy Ring to crack! Or challenge your Spy Ring to write their names using the hieroglyphs.

ACTIVE AGENTS

45 minutes

Bring everyone together so that the Agents can get active! Play the MISSION:RESCUE theme song as a sign for the children to join the larger group.

Agents X and Y should welcome the children back and ask what they enjoyed from the day before and what secret messages they wrote using the hieroglyphs (if you used that activity). Remind the children of the simple rules that you have, what to do if there's a fire and where the toilets are.

X and Y should then go on to set up the theme for the day. We hear a fairly ordinary ringtone and X pulls out a mobile phone and answers it. She chats furtively as if she is receiving a secret mission, using codewords. Shortly after we hear an outlandish ringtone and Y pulls a giant mobile (made out of a shoebox or something similar), and shouts into it. He shouts about his secret mission, giving away all the details of where he's going to meet his contact etc. After a minute, X should realise that Y is giving away all the details and try to stop him.

X explains to Y about how he's getting this spy thing all wrong. He should find the best ways to communicate with the Chief. Y thinks that bigger is better and that his giant mobile is the best tool for the job (have some fun with the 'But why, Y?!' shout here). X shows Y all the secret devices she's been given (pretending she has an X-ray watch, a listening device in her shoe or a false moustache concealed in her pocket). She shows Y her mobile and tells him how it's the best way of communicating.

Tell the children that you're going to discover how God communicates, and gives Moses all the devices he needs for the mission. Leave Y's giant mobile somewhere out of the way on the set, near the sleeping bag from Day 1.

SPY WORKOUT

The Spy Fitness Instructor (SFI) should lead a workout, reminding the Agents of the need to be fit to carry out their rescue mission! Use the simple exercises you used in the first session, adding in one or two more. Remember to include actions suitable for children with special needs, if necessary.

SPY SONGS

Reintroduce the CodeCrackers and sing the MISSION:RESCUE theme song, together with the actions. Sing another song that you sang during the first session.

OPERATION: COMMUNICATION

Today's special operation is all about passing messages, by playing charades. Before the session, prepare a list of five or six television programmes and films for the Spy Rings to act out. Explain to the Agents that a volunteer from each Spy Ring should come out to the front to see the first TV show/film on the list. They then go back to their Spy Ring and act out the TV show/ film. When one of their Spy Ring guesses the answer correctly, another member of the Ring should go to Agent X or Y to find out the next TV show/film and so on. The winning team is the first Spy Ring to guess all the TV shows/films.

Congratulate the winning Spy Ring and award points if you are using them.

SECURITY REPORT

The Head of Security comes to deliver today's report (maybe wearing a yellow T-shirt). They should make these points:

- Security level banana yellow.
- Y needs to learn to speak quietly on the phone.
- Moses is rescued as a baby, as a young man after killing an Egyptian and rescued by Jethro in the desert.
- But the people still need rescuing. How will God turn Moses into his rescue agent?

Repeat: security level banana yellow! Stay alert, Agents!

SPY CHIEF'S CLUES

Introduce the Spy Chief and ask them to reveal their clues for today. The Spy Chief should ask Q-Tech to how his clue on the screen – video footage of fire (there is a video file available on the MISSION:RESCUE website). Y can get confused and think the screen is on fire and make to put it out with a 'bucket of water' (bucket of polystyrene packaging or small pieces of paper). The Spy Chief can point out that although we can see the flames on the screen, we know that the screen is not on fire!

REVEALING THE SECRET

The Spy Chief should say goodbye to X and Y and go on to tell the story, or introduce today's episode from the MISSION:RESCUE DVD. (If you are both telling the story and using the DVD, tell the story with the clues first, then show the DVD.) The Spy Chief should tell the story in their own words or use this script (leaving the fire on the screen throughout):

So, where did we leave Moses, God's rescuer, yesterday? He had been rescued by God and was living in a land called Midian. He had a wife called Zipporah and a son called Gershom. Moses was a shepherd and looked after Jethro's sheep (Jethro was Zipporah's dad). One day, Moses was out with the sheep, wandering around the desert when he came to a mountain, called Sinai. This was the mountain of God! The sheep were roaming about all over the place and Moses was trying to round them all up when he saw something out of the corner of his eye. It wasn't a sheep, or a wolf coming to attack his flock. It was a bush. It was a bush that was on fire! **(Point to the fire on the screen.)**

Moses went up to it to get a better look. He'd seen bushes on fire before – if lightning hit one during a storm, it would burn brightly in the gloom – but this one was different. As Moses got closer, he realised what was different. Although the bush was on fire, the branches and the leaves weren't burning! Just like the fire on the screen, but this wasn't projected – it was real fire! Moses stared at the strange sight. But then, it got stranger.

'Moses, Moses!' God spoke to him! Can you believe it? God had rescued Moses and now he was talking with him. Moses replied, 'Here I am.'

'Don't come any closer,' God said, 'because you're standing on holy ground. Take off your sandals. I am the God of your ancestors!' Moses hid his face, because he was afraid to look at God, and he took off his sandals. **(Take off your shoes, and hide your face, as if you were Moses.)**

God carried on speaking: 'I have seen how unhappy my people are in Egypt, the tough times they are going through. I know how much they hurt. I will rescue them from Egypt and give them a new home – a country where there's lots of space to grow food and keep animals. Go, Moses! You are to lead my people out of Egypt.'

Moses was really scared! 'I can't do that!' he cried. 'I'm not a great man, I can't go to the king of Egypt, the pharaoh, and tell him to let the Israelites go!'

God knew that Moses was worried. 'I'll be with you,' he said. 'I'll give you the words to say. I AM WHO I AM. When you speak to them, tell them, "I AM sent me." They'll believe you and follow you.'

Then God told Moses what to say to the Israelites. He was going to send Moses to rescue them, and he would be with Moses every step of the way. But Moses was still nervous. He didn't want to go, but God showed him things that persuaded him that God would be there, including a wooden walking stick that God turned into a snake! Finally God promised that Moses' brother Aaron would go with him to see Pharaoh. Moses would be accompanied by both God and Aaron! God had given Moses all he needed!

(Point to the fire again.) So God had spoken to Moses in a special way and given him the rescue mission! God didn't expect Moses to be completely unprepared. He told Moses what to say and gave him everything he needed. What's next for Moses and the rescue mission? We'll have to wait and see!

CHECKING THE EVIDENCE

X and Y should thank the Spy Chief, then introduce the quiz. Before the session, put together some questions about the story, and also include some that are about the other parts of the morning so far (eg the workout or Operation: communication). You could include:

- Why was Y not being a good spy? (He was giving away all the secrets of his secret meeting.)
- What was Moses' job in Midian? (A shepherd.)
- What was special about the bush Moses saw? (It was on fire, but not burning up.)
- What did Moses have to do when he was standing by the bush? (Take his sandals off.)

As yesterday, make the quiz quick and lively, so the children have a chance to review the story and let off some steam after sitting and listening. Introduce the point-awarding gadget and use it to award points (see page 10).

TODAY'S MISSION

After the quiz, X and Y should briefly review the day's story, talking through these points:

- God knew how unhappy his people were in Egypt, and took the next step to rescue them.
- God spoke to Moses and he listened to him too. Moses was able to tell God how he felt.
- God knew what Moses needed, and he made sure that Moses got everything that would be necessary when he went back to Egypt – a message for the Israelites, a special walking stick, his brother to speak to the pharaoh because Moses was too nervous to.
- God speaks to us today too! And he listens. It's called prayer, we can talk to him anytime, and we know that he listens to us. He also gives us everything we need to do the things that he has in store for us. He never forgets anything.

THE GODCODE

Tell the children that you are going to talk to God, to pray now. Like Moses told God how he felt, we can tell God how we feel. Remind the Agents about the spy prayer action from the previous session and then say a simple prayer, thanking God that he talks to us, and that he listens. Tell the children to think about what they might want to say to God now – they might be feeling scared about something, like Moses did. Leave a short time of quiet for children to talk to God about this.

SPY SONGS

Sing the MISSION:RESCUE theme song again, together with one or two songs that reflect the theme of the day. You could choose:

- 'Be bold, be strong' kidsource (Kevin Mayhew Ltd)
- 'God's people aren't super-brave super heroes' kidsource (Kevin Mayhew Ltd)

After the songs, introduce the Interrogation section, where Agents will be able to question a member of the Secret Service. Encourage the Spy Rings to think of questions to ask that SSM. Then send everyone to their spy bases to explore the story more.

GOING UNDERCOVER

45 minutes

THE MAD LABORATORY

Serve your chosen refreshments and chat together about the club so far. What are the children's favourite parts? Remind the Ring to think of questions for today's interrogation and write them down for Agents X and Y to ask later. Remind them also of the dead letter drop, where they can leave their jokes and pictures. Go on to explore the Bible passage together more closely.

BIBLE DISCOVERY

With older children

Get the children thinking about ways to communicate by guessing what the pictures are on page 11 of Secret Files. Dig into the story of Exodus 3 by reading the Bible passage on pages 12 and 13 and underlining God's and Moses' parts in the right colour. Help the children to think about what Moses might have felt, then encourage them to draw in how he felt on the three faces.

Chat together about how God communicated with Moses. Chat about how God talks with us today. Be ready to tell a story of how God has talked with you recently. Then help the children write or draw what they want to say to God on pages 14 and 15, especially things they might be worried about. Don't forget to return to these pages later in the week to see if God has answered the prayers. You could also use these pages throughout the week to record any prayers you have prayed in MISSION:RESCUE.

Finally, crack the codes on page 16 to find out what God gave Moses to help him on the mission. You may want to briefly retell what happens in Exodus 4, so that the children can see how these things all fit into God's plan.

With younger children

Look at the pictures on Spy Sheet 2 and try to decide what these methods of communication are. Go on to read the Bible passage to the children, trying to be as expressive and descriptive as you can be in your reading. Try to bring some of the awe of the burning bush and God speaking to Moses, and something of what Moses must have been feeling.

When you have finished, decide together which picture fits the story the best, and ask the children what they think of the story. If appropriate, write down some of their thoughts. Go on to crack the codes (the answers are 'rescue', 'Egypt', 'eternal' and 'I AM'). You may need to explain what eternal means and then go on to wonder together what the name 'I AM' means.

Chat together about things the children might want to pray about, and tell them of a time when you have been given everything you needed by God. Spend some time praying together about anything the children would like to. If you have time, retell the story of Exodus 4:1–17.

With all age groups

Adapt these questions to suit your group, sharing your own feelings, opinions and experiences as appropriate:

- How do you think Moses felt when he saw the burning bush?
- How do you think Moses felt when he realised God was speaking to him?
- How did God try to make Moses feel better about going on the mission?
- What do you think the name 'I AM' means?
- Moses told God how he felt. What would you like to say to God? He listens and speaks to us, just as he did to Moses (though probably not from a burning bush).

Q-TECH'S WORKSHOP

Choose something to make (a construction activity) from Q-Tech's spy store (see page 27), deciding whether to do an individual or an all-together construction. For extra ideas, see Ultimate Craft (SU, 978 1 84427 364 5).

SPIES' TIME OUT

Help the Agents let off steam by choosing suitable games from Q-Tech's spy store (see page 27). See page 10 for more info about choosing the best games for your club. For extra games ideas, check out Ultimate Games (SU, 978 1 84427 365 2).

AGENTS ARE GO!

25 minutes

DEAD LETTER DROP

Welcome everyone back together by playing the MISSION:RESCUE theme song. Read out some of the secret messages and pictures from the dead letter drop. Thank all the contributing Agents and remind everyone to bring in more jokes and pictures tomorrow.

SPY SONGS

The CodeCrackers lead a song that you have already sung at the club.

RETURN OF THE SPY CHIEF

Welcome back the Spy Chief, who goes on to round up what the Spy Rings have been exploring together. The Spy Chief should sum up these points:

- With the fire on the screen: God talked to Moses using something very unusual! Moses was able to tell God how he felt. We can talk to God too, any time we like; we don't have to wait for the burning bush. And God can talk to us any time too!
- God was going to use Moses as his rescuer! He said words to Moses that would make him feel better: that he was always going to be with him, that he was the everlasting God and that his name is 'I AM'!
- God went on to give Moses everything he needed for the mission – his stick to do miracles, the words to say and his brother to say them! God will give us everything we need for our missions too.

INTERROGATION

Introduce the Secret Service member who is to be interrogated. Before the session, go through with the SSM what you're going to talk about – how God has spoken to them, and maybe how God has given them things that they needed – making sure that their story is appropriate. Interrogate the SSM, including some of the questions the children have thought of. When you have finished, thank the SSM for being willing to be interrogated!

DRAMA: WHO'S THE MOLE?

Introduce the next episode of the drama: 'Who's the mole?' Today the mole keeps changing the agents' instructions by switching words round in the messages. Then the mole plots to steal some of the top secret equipment!

CRACKING THE CODE

With the help of the CodeCrackers, carry on learning the Learn and remember verse for MISSION:RESCUE – Psalm 118:24 – by singing the Learn and remember verse song. If you're not using the song, text a version

of the Bible verse with some of the words missing to the Spymasters. The Spy Rings should work together to fill in the blanks on the message.

COMPLETING THE MISSION

Round off Agents are go! by asking the children what they have enjoyed at MISSION:RESCUE today and then include those things in a short prayer of thanks, using your spy prayer action (and shout). Sing the MISSION:RESCUE theme song and send the Agents back to their Spy Rings to round off the day's session.

AGENTS' DEBRIEF

10 minutes

As you sit together for the final time today, chat about the highlights of the day. Finish any pages of Secret Files or sections of the Spy Sheets you have not done, or carry on with the construction or activity from Agents' briefing. Alternatively, pray together using this prayer activity:

CHAT WITH GOD

What you need

☐ An object (a soft toy or ball, or something more spy-related such as dark glasses or a mobile phone)

What you do

Gather the children together in a circle and ask them to think of something they are worried about that they'd like to tell God. If you have a chatty Spy Ring, they might want to tell you what that is, but don't force anyone to tell the group. Show your object and explain that you're going to pass it round the group. When an Agent holds the object, it's their turn to pray. Let the group know that they can pray out loud or in their heads. Round off the time of prayer by thanking God that he heard Moses and that he hears us too.

As the children are picked up from their Spy Rings, make sure they are reminded of the next session, and that they take all of their belongings with them. Make sure too that they remember to bring in jokes, pictures and questions for the dead letter drop. Each Spymaster should know how each of the children in their group is getting home.

MISSION CLEAR-UP

30 minutes

After all the children have gone, clear up from the day's events and set up for the next session. Meet together as a team to debrief. Continue to feed back what is working and what might need tweaking. Have a brief time of prayer where everyone together prays for the whole club, thanking God for what he has done so far and telling him of any concerns you have. If you have the time and the facilities, you may wish to share a meal together.

SPY SHEET 2
Your mission...

Can you spot these ways of talking to people? Which ones do you use in your family?

  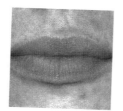  

Listen to the story and decide which of these pictures best fit how God spoke to Moses.

Crack these codes to find out what God told Moses.

I have come to _ _ _ _ _ _
them from _ _ _ _ _ .

I am the _ _ _ _ _ _ _ God.

My name is "_ _   _ _ _".

KEYCODE

✖	●	▶	@	🏃	✚	■	✳	◆	❎	∂	🦈	⋉	★	❓	📞	⊖	🐤	⚡	🏰	♣	✦	❞	☹	⊕	🍃
A	B	C	D	E	F	G	H	I	J	K	L	M	N	O	P	Q	R	S	T	U	V	W	X	Y	Z

Moses was still scared, but God gave him everything he needed to carry out the mission. Ask your Spymaster about a time when God gave them what they needed.

MISSION 3

Mission abort?

Mission briefing

SPIRITUAL PREPARATION

READ TOGETHER

Retell briefly the story of Exodus 5:1–21 and then go on to read 5:22 – 6:13 together.

EXPLORE TOGETHER

Split the team into smaller groups (for example, pairs or threes). Ask all the groups to look at Exodus 5:22 – 6:13. Ask everyone to reflect on and discuss these questions:

- What do you think of Moses' response to God, following his meeting with Pharaoh and Pharaoh's subsequent actions?
- How does God respond? Does this surprise you?
- If you were in Moses' place, what would you think?
- What part does this story play in God's wider rescue mission for his people?

When all the groups have finished, gather back together and feed back the thoughts of each group.

REFLECT TOGETHER

After the drama of the past two days, this story seems a bit of an anti-climax. Moses and Aaron arrive at Pharaoh's court to deliver God's message, but Pharaoh turns them down flat. In fact, he makes the Israelites' lives worse because of Moses' actions. Where does this leave God's rescue mission? Moses' reaction in 5:22 and 23 is probably typical of how we all would have felt in his place. After meeting God so powerfully in chapters 3 and 4, he hits a low when he returns to Egypt and things don't go the way he expects.

It's tough for Moses, as he doesn't know exactly what God has planned. God's mission was going to last a lot longer than Moses must have expected.

KEY PASSAGE
Exodus 5:1–21 (retold); 5:22 – 6:13

KEY AIMS

- to find out that God is in control, even when it doesn't look like it
- to continue to build relationships with the children, and to welcome those who are new to the club today

KEY STORY
Moses starts his mission, but isn't able to persuade Pharaoh to let the Israelites go. Pharaoh makes life worse because of Moses' actions, but God promises that he will rescue his people. The confrontation begins!

For children with no church background
All children will be familiar with the feeling that things aren't going their way. They often aren't in control of what happens in their lives. It can sometimes seem that, even when they think everything is in place, their desired outcome never happens. Use this story to help them think about how powerful God is, and that he always keeps his promises, even when it doesn't go how we want it to go.

For church children
Children who have grown up in church may have been told many times that God will be there for them and is control, but they may never have experienced that in a negative situation, such as Moses does here. This story may surprise them, as they encounter a story where it seems God is not working. Help them grasp the idea that God's mission may not follow the course that we think it should. God is in control, even though we may not understand his plan.

For children from other faiths
Understanding God's activity in the world is a challenge for people of all faiths. Muslims might well say that even if it isn't going their way it is the will of Allah. 'Inshallah' means God willing and is often said by Muslims when talking of future events. 'I'll come to the club tomorrow, inshallah.' For some Hindus and Buddhists, when things don't go your way it is bad karma. Something's happening because of something bad you've done in this (or a previous) life.

For children with additional needs
Children with Down's syndrome often have a 'black and white' way of reacting to situations. If something is difficult there may be loud crying or running away to 'hide' under somewhere such as a table. Give the child space for a short time and then approach with confidence and humour. Ignore the behaviour if possible using positive 'I' statements to say what you would like to happen, for instance: 'I would like you to sit next to Josh so everyone can enjoy the story.'

Moses knows God is all-powerful and could rescue the people in a moment, but God has more to do than Moses knows about. As we will find out, the plagues God sends on Egypt proclaim who he is, both to Egypt and to Israel. And if the mission succeeded straight away, those lessons would not have been learned.

How do we react when God's plans do not seem to come about straight away? What do we think when events turn away from the course we think they should take? Reread some of God's promise to Moses and the Israelites in chapter 6 – if God promises to do something, he WILL do it. We have to be patient.

PRAY TOGETHER

- Pray for the children you know are coming today by name, and pray for those not yet registered who will turn up at the door.
- Pray for the events you have planned today.
- Pray that God will help you and the children reflect more about following God's plans and sticking with his promises, even though things aren't working out as we think they should. If this brings up issues for any leaders, make sure this is picked up outside club time.
- Pray for continuing friendships, that you will be able to work towards lasting relationships with the children and their families.
- Pray for each other, about any specific worries or needs that you have. Pray also that God will give you everything you need as you work for him.

PRACTICAL PREPARATION

Talk through your programme together, ensuring that everyone knows their part in the day and has everything they need. Set up the different areas of the club and make sure that everything is in place. Make sure you make any adjustments you agreed in your evaluation session after the previous session. Encourage the team to continue welcoming the children (and their families if possible), working to build lasting relationships.

WHAT YOU NEED CHECKLIST

- ☐ **Registration** Registration forms, badges, labels, pens, team lists
- ☐ **Spy Rings** Bibles, Secret Files or Spy Sheets, Bible discovery notes, pens and pencils
- ☐ **Music** The CodeCrackers band or backing tracks
- ☐ **Drama** Costume and props
- ☐ **Q-Tech** PA system, laptop, PowerPoints and projection/OHP and acetates, MISSION:RESCUE DVD
- ☐ **Activities** Equipment for games and construction
- ☐ **Agents X and Y** Running order, notes, quiz questions, two remote control cars, one spare remote control car control, Operation: remote control equipment
- ☐ **The mad laboratory** Drinks and biscuits, or other refreshments
- ☐ **Spy Chief** story script, secret message, a volunteer to play Aaron, suitable Old Testament costume and stick for Aaron, toy rubber snake

On the mission

As the children arrive and register, play some spy-themed music (such as Bond or Mission Impossible theme tunes) and display the MISSION:RESCUE logo on the screen to welcome the children.

Have plenty of the team available in the registration area to welcome any new children, to chat to parents and to make sure everyone knows where they are going. Spymasters and Assistants should be ready in their bases to welcome and chat with their Agents.

AGENTS' BRIEFING

10 minutes

As the children arrive, if you started the spy base activity in the first session, carry on working together to create your base. Otherwise try this activity.

SILENT SIGNALS

What you need
- ☐ Pencils and paper

What you do

Encourage your Spy Ring to come up with some signals that they can use to communicate with each other. You could use different arm positions to mean different things. For example, folding arms could mean 'yes', scratching your nose 'no' or one hand in a pocket 'I'm being followed'. You could also use leg movement, winking or hand signals to create a method of communication. Write down the signals and then practise them – see if you can communicate with each other!

ACTIVE AGENTS

45 minutes

Bring everyone together so that the Agents can get active! Play the MISSION:RESCUE theme song as a sign for the children to join the larger group.

Agents X and Y should welcome the children back and ask what they enjoyed from the day before. You could invite some Spy Rings to show you their secret communications. Remind the children of the simple rules you have, what to do if there's a fire and where the toilets are.

X tells Y about the new way they have to deliver messages. They can use this method to sneak messages into places without being noticed. X shows Y the two remote control cars, with messages attached to them. X should give Y one of the cars and the spare remote control, while keeping a correct car/control combination for herself. The controller for Y's car should be given before the session starts to a member of the Secret Service at the back of your hall. X demonstrates how to deliver a message by directing her car to one of the Spymasters. Y then has a go, but of course his controller won't work. The SSM should send Y's car in completely the wrong direction. After a couple of goes, Y complains that he isn't in control of the car and that this is a stupid way to communicate. Then Y realises that someone else is in control of his car!

X should reassure Y and leave Y's car and control next to the sleeping bag and mobile phone from Days 1 and 2. She should then challenge the children to see if they can deliver messages better than Y in today's special operation.

SPY WORKOUT

The Spy Fitness Instructor (SFI) should lead the workout. Introduce a couple of new activities and invite some volunteers to come and help lead the workout. Everyone needs to be in the best shape to carry out their missions!

SPY SONGS

Reintroduce the CodeCrackers and sing the MISSION: RESCUE theme song, together with the actions. Sing one or two other songs that you have already sung at MISSION:RESCUE.

OPERATION: REMOTE CONTROL

Ask for a few volunteers to complete today's special operation – delivering messages with the remote control cars (choose as many volunteers as you have cars). Set up a simple set of obstacles on your stage for the cars to go round to deliver their message to one of the Spymasters at the end of the course. Give each volunteer a control and car, and explain the rules to them. Encourage the Agents to cheer for the volunteers and then see who can get their message round the obstacles the quickest! Award points to the Agents, if you are keeping score.

SECURITY REPORT

The Head of Security comes to deliver today's report. They should make these points:
- Security level Barbie pink.
- Y loses his driving licence!
- Moses is rescued as a baby, as a young man after killing an Egyptian and rescued by Jethro in the desert.
- Moses meets God and is given everything he needs for the rescue mission.
- Moses and Aaron are on their way to see Pharaoh. Will they be successful?

Repeat: security level Barbie pink! Stay alert, Agents!

SPY CHIEF'S CLUES

Introduce the Spy Chief and ask them to reveal their clue for today. The Spy Chief reveals a secret message he has received from an agent who is on a mission. He should read it out (as he reads, put it up on the screen too – see the MISSION:RESCUE website for a PowerPoint slide):

My first is in bag, but not in bus
My second repeat
My third is all around us
My fourth is in moths but not in maths
My fifth starts nice, naughty then nasty
Meet me alone at MISSION:RESCUE!
(Answers: A, A, R [air], O, N)

X and Y try to work out who he is. Try to make this as comic and inept as possible (with plenty of 'But why, Y?!' Y could try to work out whose name starts 'GG', keep repeating 'My second' because he thinks that line is an instruction or wonder what starts out nice, then gets more badly behaved. Finally X and Y work out (with the children helping if they can) that the agent is Aaron. The Chief should get X and Y to go, as he has to meet Aaron alone (the children can stay though!).

REVEALING THE SECRET

The Spy Chief should say goodbye to X and Y and go on to tell the story, or introduce today's episode from the MISSION:RESCUE DVD. (If you are telling the story and using the DVD, tell the story with the clues first, then show the DVD.) The Spy Chief should tell the story in their own words or use this script (this will work best if the Chief and Aaron have had time to rehearse):

Chief: (To children.) I wonder when Aaron will turn up. You'll let me know, won't you?

Aaron arrives stealthily round the back of the stage. The children may start to shout 'Behind you' or similar.

Aaron and the Chief should keep missing each other, until Aaron taps the Chief on the shoulder, giving him a fright.

Aaron: Chief, I'm here!

Chief: (Shouting.) Aaron, it's you!

Aaron: Sssh! Don't tell everyone I'm here!

Chief: (Whispering.) Sorry! Good to see you. What did you want to tell us?

Aaron: I wanted to let you know how the mission was going on.

Chief: Fantastic! All the agents know how your brother Moses met God and God gave him the mission, and everything he needed – including you! So, how's it going? You must have succeeded by now!

Aaron: Well, no actually, it's not going well.

Chief: What? But I thought God was with you both, and that he wanted to rescue his people from Egypt!

Aaron: He does! But the mission's not going how we thought it would. You see, I met Moses when he came back from Midian and we went to see Pharaoh. We told him what God told us to say: 'Let my people go into the desert so that they can worship me.'

Chief: And what did Pharaoh say?

Aaron: No.

Chief: He said no? How could he do that?

Aaron: He said, 'Who is your God? No, I will not let your people go!'

Chief: What did you do then?

Aaron: Well, we told him again, and that God wouldn't be happy if we didn't go, but Pharaoh still said no. In fact, he was really angry and accused us of making trouble. 'Moses and Aaron,' he said, 'you are stopping the Israelites from working. They are building my temples and my cities. If they leave, nothing will get finished. Now get back to work!'

Chief: Wow! I thought God's rescue mission would be sorted really quickly!

Aaron: So did I, but Pharaoh hasn't finished being nasty. After we had left, he told his slave masters that they should take away the Israelites' straw.

Chief: Their straw?

Aaron: Yes. The Israelites make bricks for Pharaoh; they need straw and clay to make them. Pharaoh stopped giving them the straw they need, so they had to find it themselves. The Israelites had to work harder and they were very unhappy. They blamed us for what Pharaoh has done.

Chief: But that's not fair! Don't they know you're on God's mission to rescue them?

Aaron: They didn't seem to remember that. Moses was really sad. He's talked to God about it. He was really honest! He said, 'Why did you send me here? Ever since I went to Pharaoh, there's been nothing but trouble. You haven't done a thing to help!'

Chief: Wow, Moses must have been really upset. What did God say? Was he angry?

Aaron: No, that's the cool thing about it. God told Moses, 'Soon you will see what is happening. Pharaoh will let my people go, because he will see how powerful I am. I'm in control of everything. I am the Lord! The Israelites will be my friends and I will be their God. I will give them a good place to live – the place I promised to your ancestors.'

Chief: That's a brilliant thing for God to say!

Aaron: Yes, God's going to keep his promise to rescue us. We just have to trust him and follow his plans. God told Moses to go back to Pharaoh.

Chief: Back to Pharaoh! Scary!

Aaron: Yes! Especially after what he did last time! But God told Moses what to say, and Moses told me. We both went to see Pharaoh. But the king demanded a miracle – he told us to do something special! So I took Moses' special stick and threw it on the ground (**He throws his stick on the floor.**) And guess what? It turned into a snake! (**He pulls out a toy rubber snake.**) But Pharaoh wasn't impressed. He said 'No! I won't let your people go!' He won't change his mind.

Chief: So what's going to happen next?

Aaron: We have to wait for God to show us, but we can trust him because he's still in control. He is going to rescue his people and nothing Pharaoh can do will stop him.

Chief: Well, thanks for the update, Aaron; we can't wait to find out what God's going to do next. You're right. God's really powerful and we have to follow him on the mission! Take care and stay safe, Aaron!

Aaron: Bye, Chief! Bye, Agents!

Aaron sneaks off the back of the stage before X and Y return.

CHECKING THE EVIDENCE

X and Y should return to the stage and ask the Spy Chief how his conversation with Aaron went. After the Chief leaves, X and Y move on to the quiz. Before the session, put together some questions about the story, and also include some that are about the other parts of the morning so far (eg the workout or Operation remote control). You could include:

- Why was Y frustrated at the start of the club? (His car wouldn't go in the direction he wanted it to.)
- What did Pharaoh say to Moses and Aaron, when they asked him to let the Israelites go? ('Who is this God?' or 'No, I won't let them go.')
- What else did Pharaoh do? (Took away the Israelites' straw.)
- What did Aaron's stick turn into? (A snake.)

As always, make the quiz quick and lively, so the children have a chance to review the story and let off some steam after sitting and listening. Bring out the point-scoring gadget with some ceremony and reverence! Then use it to award points.

TODAY'S MISSION

After the quiz, X and Y should review the day's story, talking through these points:

- Pharaoh didn't listen to Moses and Aaron and made the Israelites' lives worse because of what Moses and Aaron did. Moses didn't understand what was going on.
- We learnt yesterday that Moses was able to tell God what he really felt and thought and he did the same again today.
- God reminded Moses of his promise to rescue his people. Moses had to accept that God knew what he was doing and, although things weren't going how he expected, God was in control. Moses and the Israelites could depend on God.
- Sometimes things don't go the way we want them to, and it can be hard to understand why. But we can always depend on God – he is in control, he knows what we need and he understands how we feel.

THE GODCODE

Tell the children that you are going to talk to God, to pray now. Remind the Agents about the spy prayer action and practise it now. Ask the children to think about a time when things weren't going the way they wanted (give a couple of examples to help the children work out what they might think of). As the children think of those times, pray that you would all remember that God is in control and that he knows how we feel. Ask him to help you understand a bit more of his plans and to help you be a part of God's mission!

SPY SONGS

Sing the MISSION:RESCUE theme song again, together with one or two songs that reflect the theme of the day. You could choose:

- 'Moses went down to see Pharaoh' kidsource (Kevin Mayhew)
- 'King of all' Reach up! (SU)

After the songs, remind everyone about the Interrogation section, where Agents will be able to question a member of the Secret Service. Encourage the Spy Rings to think of questions to ask that SSM. Then send everyone to their spy bases to explore the story more.

GOING UNDERCOVER
45 minutes

THE MAD LABORATORY

Serve your chosen refreshments and chat together about the club so far. What did the children think of today's story? Remind the Ring to think of questions for today's interrogation and write them down for Agents X and Y to ask later. Remind them also of the dead letter drop, where they can leave their jokes and pictures. Go on to explore the Bible passage together more closely.

BIBLE DISCOVERY
With older children

Start to think about times when things do not go according to plan by doing the activity on page 17 of Secret Files. Give the children time to reflect on this and to write or draw it in the space provided. Share some of the ideas if the children want to, and maybe give an example from your own life. Go on to read the passage (either from a Bible or on pages 18 and 19). Using chapter 5 verses 22 and 23, choose the words that best describe Moses. If the children have their own suggestions, write them on the page too. Read the rest of the passage and help the group answer the simple questions. Chat about why Moses might have been cheered up by God's message – Moses thinks things haven't gone well, but God tells him that he's in control, he has mighty power!

Encourage the children to think about Moses' response to this. What would he tell Jethro, if he were to write him an email about his visit to Pharaoh and God's message? Allow the children time to write their emails on pages 20 and 21. Chat through anything the children would like to discuss, relating to what they have written or about the story.

Pray about what you have discovered using the activity on page 22. If you have time, go on to the story of Aaron's walking stick turning into a snake on page 23.

With younger children

Read the Bible verse together and help the children to draw, then write what they think is happening at each point in the story on Spy Sheet 3. Once everyone has finished, get the children to retell the story to each other (if you did this on Day 1 and it didn't work particularly well, miss it out).

Try to help the children think about how Moses must have felt during this part of the story. Use the words on the Spy Sheet to help them think about it. How did Moses' mood change before and after meeting Pharaoh? What about when he complained to God? And what about after hearing what God had to say? Alternatively, draw a long line on a piece of paper and write 'Very happy' at one end and 'Very sad' at the other. Get the children to point to a place on the line to represent Moses at each point in the story.

Finally, chat about God having a plan and being in control even when things seem to be going wrong. Things didn't go right for Moses straight away, but God was still in control. Ask the children to reflect on any times in their life when things have gone wrong and write or draw in the speech bubble what they want to say to God.

With all age groups

Adapt these questions to suit your group, sharing your own feelings, opinions and experiences as appropriate:

- After meeting God and being given everything he needed for the mission, how do you think Moses felt before meeting Pharaoh? And afterwards?
- Was Moses right to complain to God like he did?
- What do you think of God's reply? What does this tell you about God?
- How can we apply this to our lives? What do we think when things don't go 'right' in our lives? Do we think that God is in control?

Q-TECH'S WORKSHOP

Choose a construction activity from Q-Tech's spy store (see page 27), deciding whether to do an individual or an all-together construction. For extra ideas, see Ultimate Craft (SU, 978 1 84427 364 5).

SPIES' TIME OUT

Help the Agents let off steam by choosing suitable games from Q-Tech's spy store (see page 27). See page 10 for more info about choosing the best games for your club. For extra games ideas, check out Ultimate Games (SU, 978 1 84427 365 2).

AGENTS ARE GO!
25 minutes

DEAD LETTER DROP

Welcome everyone back together by playing the MISSION:RESCUE theme song. Read out some of the secret messages and pictures from the dead letter drop. Thank all the contributing Agents and remind everyone to bring in more jokes and pictures tomorrow.

SPY SONGS

The CodeCrackers lead a song that you have already sung to start this all-together section.

RETURN OF THE SPY CHIEF

Welcome back the Spy Chief, who goes on to round up what the Spy Rings have been exploring together. The Spy Chief should sum up these points:

- Moses has everything he needs for the mission, but it seems to go wrong! Pharaoh ignores Moses and makes the Israelites' lives worse.
- God is in control. He reminds Moses that he is God – 'I AM'! He tells Moses about his promise to rescue his people. He has not forgotten the mission, and it hasn't gone wrong!
- (Picking up Y's controller from Active agents.) Sometimes we can feel like things aren't going right, like Y and his remote control car! But God is in control and he has a plan – even when things seem like they're not going right. We can talk to God about it and trust him.

INTERROGATION

Introduce the Secret Service member who is to be interrogated. Before the session, go through with the SSM what you're going to talk about – about a time when, even though things were going wrong, God was still in control, and how God worked out his plan – making sure that their story is appropriate. Interrogate the SSM, including some of the questions the children have thought of. When you have finished, thank the SSM for being willing to be interrogated!

DRAMA: WHO'S THE MOLE?

Introduce the next episode of the drama: 'Who's the mole?' Today the mole's sabotage works so well that all the agents' plans seem like they're ruined! The team are very unhappy, but will they find out who the mole is?

CRACKING THE CODE

With the help of the CodeCrackers, carry on learning the Learn and remember verse for MISSION:RESCUE

– Psalm 118:24 – by singing the Learn and remember verse song.

If you're not using the song, write the words of the verse on balloons. Give each balloon to a volunteer and challenge all the Agents to arrange the words in the right order. Then say the verse together. Keep saying the verse, but pop a few balloons before each time (warning children who may find balloon-popping unpleasant – alternatively, you could simply put the balloons out of sight).

COMPLETING THE MISSION

Round off Agents are go! by asking the children what they have enjoyed at MISSION:RESCUE today and then include those things in a short prayer of thanks, using your spy prayer action (and shout). Sing the MISSION: RESCUE theme song and send the Agents back to their Spy Rings to round off the day's session.

AGENTS' DEBRIEF

10 minutes

As you sit together for the final time today, chat about the highlights of the day. Finish any pages of Secret Files or sections of the Spy Sheets you have not done, or carry on with the construction or activity from Agents' briefing. Alternatively, pray together using this prayer activity:

CHAT WITH GOD

What you need
- ☐ Large sheet of paper with 'God's mighty power' written on it
- ☐ Sticky notes and pens

What you do

Gather the children in a circle and place the large sheet of paper in the middle. Give each Agent a pen and a couple of sticky notes and ask them to think about things they want to say to God. Are there situations in their lives where they'd like to know God's in control? Is there any situation where they'd like him to show his mighty power? Get them to write or draw on the stickies what they want to say (helping out where necessary), and fix the notes to the paper. When everyone has finished, use some of the sticky notes to round up the time of prayer, asking God to help us see that he's in control.

As the children are picked up from their Spy Rings, make sure they are reminded of the next session, and that they take all of their belongings with them. Make sure too that they remember to bring in jokes, pictures

and questions for the dead letter drop. Each Spymaster should know how each of the children in their group is getting home.

MISSION CLEAR UP

30 minutes

After all the children have gone, clear up from the day's events and set up for the next session. Meet together as a team to debrief. Continue to feed back what is working and what might need tweaking. Have a brief time of prayer where everyone together prays for the whole club, thanking God for what he has done so far and lifting up any concerns to him. If you have the time and the facilities, you may wish to share a meal together.

SPY SHEET 3
Mission abort?

Read these Bible verses and draw what is happening in the boxes!

Exodus 5:1–2	**Exodus 5:22–23**	**Exodus 6:1–2,5**

Which of these words can you use to describe Moses? Circle the ones you think describe him.

Happy

Sad

Excited

Naughty

Angry

Upset

Sorry

Not bothered

Chat with your group about the words you chose.

Sometimes, we think things have gone wrong and we don't know why. But Moses learnt that God was always in control. The mission wasn't going well, but God had a plan to rescue his people.

In this speech bubble, write or draw what you think.

MISSION 4

Mission accomplished

Mission briefing

SPIRITUAL PREPARATION

READ TOGETHER
Briefly retell the story of Exodus 7–10, or look at the plague infographic on the MISSION:RESCUE website. Then go on to read Exodus 11; 12:29–42 together.

EXPLORE TOGETHER
Split the team into two. Ask one group to look at Exodus 11; 12:29–32 and the other to look at Exodus 12:33–42. Ask everyone to reflect on and discuss these questions:
- What is God doing in this passage?
- How does this represent the success of God's rescue mission?
- If you were in Moses' place, what would you think? When both the groups have finished, gather back together and feed back the thoughts of each group.

REFLECT TOGETHER
Today's Bible stories contain the whole range of God's punishment on Pharaoh, from the blood of the Nile to the death of the firstborn. Faced with so much suffering, it is difficult to keep focused on God's plan. Each one of the plagues attacked Egypt's economy, power and religion, with God mocking Egypt's false gods by demonstrating dominion over their 'responsibilities'. God was stating his power over everything, including Egypt and the pharaoh, while at the same time showing Israel that he is God.

Eventually pharaoh releases the Israelites, but only after he has been struck personally – his heir, his hope for the continuing power of Egypt (and his legacy) has been killed. He has paid for his pride with the life of his son. The plagues leave interesting questions about suffering and deserved punishment – why should the whole of Egypt suffer for the pharaoh's pride? Give yourself time to reflect on these questions before the club.

However, the sacrifice of the Passover lamb to save the firstborn of the Israelites (and bring about the success of God's rescue mission) is a great positive, an indication of God's ultimate rescue mission – that of Jesus' sacrifice. What is your response to Jesus' actions on the cross? How much difference does it make to you? Be prepared to emphasise this today, as some children hear the good news for the first time!

PRAY TOGETHER
- Pray for the children you know are coming today by name, and pray for those not yet registered who will turn up at the door.
- Pray for the events you have planned today and that you get the right tone for the session, balancing seriousness with positive points.
- Pray that God would reveal his ultimate salvation mission to the children today.
- Pray for continuing friendships, that you will be able to work towards lasting relationships with the children and their families.
- Pray for each other, about any specific worries or needs that you have. Pray also that God will give you everything you need as you work for him.

PRACTICAL PREPARATION
Talk through your programme together, ensuring that everyone knows their part in the day and has everything they need. Set up the different areas of the club and make sure that everything is in place. Make sure you make any adjustments you agreed in your evaluation session after the previous session. Encourage the team to continue welcoming the children (and their families if possible), working to build lasting relationships.

WHAT YOU NEED CHECKLIST

- ☐ **Registration** Registration forms, badges, labels, pens, team lists
- ☐ **Spy Rings** Bibles, Secret Files or Spy Sheets, Bible discovery notes, pens and pencils, code wheel resources
- ☐ **Music** The CodeCrackers band or backing tracks
- ☐ **Drama** Costume and props
- ☐ **Q-Tech** PA system, laptop, PowerPoints and projection/OHP and acetates, MISSION:RESCUE DVD
- ☐ **Activities** Equipment for games and construction
- ☐ **Agents X and Y** Running order, notes, quiz questions, Operation: gunge rescue resources
- ☐ **The mad laboratory** Drinks and biscuits, or other refreshments
- ☐ **Spy Chief** Story script, secret message, cue cards for the story (see the MISSION:RESCUE website)

On the mission

As the children arrive and register, play some spy-themed music (such as Bond or Mission Impossible theme tunes) and display the MISSION:RESCUE logo on the screen to welcome the children.

Have plenty of the team available in the registration area to welcome any new children, to chat to parents and to make sure everyone knows where they are going. Spymasters and Assistants should be ready in their bases to welcome and chat with their Agents.

AGENTS' BRIEFING

10 minutes

As the children arrive, if you started the spy base activity in the first session, carry on working together to create your base. Otherwise try this activity.

CODE WHEEL

What you need

- ☐ Code wheel sheet for each Agent (see page 35)
- ☐ Scissors
- ☐ Spilt pins (paper fasteners)
- ☐ Pens and paper

What you do

Give out the code wheel sheet and encourage the Agents to cut out the two circles (if you have a young group, you may wish to provide pre-cut circles). Show the group how to fasten the two wheels together with a split pin. Show the group how to set the wheel to code G (set the G on the

KEY PASSAGE

Exodus 7–10 (retold)
Exodus 11; 12:29–32,33–42

KEY AIMS

- to explore what it means that God rescues and saves, and to respond to God's rescue mission
- to continue to build relationships with the children, and to introduce Jesus to children with little or no church background

KEY STORY

After the first nine plagues, God's final plague on the Egyptians finally forces Pharaoh to let the people go. God's words are not empty – he does what he says he will do. God's people are saved by sacrificing a lamb and spreading its blood on their doorposts. They share the first Passover together, celebrating God's rescue.

For children with no church background

Today, the story of God's rescue and the sacrifice at Passover brings with it the story of God's ultimate rescue mission – Jesus. Make sure, in this packed story, that you spend enough time introducing the story of Jesus' rescue to children with little or no church background. Allow time for children to respond to the fact that God keeps his promises and to Jesus' ultimate rescue.

For church children

Church children may well have encountered the story of the plagues before and the seriousness of what God does may have lost some of its impact. When you come to talking about Jesus' sacrifice, try to encourage church children to reflect on that. Familiarity can bring apathy towards this ultimate rescue mission!

For children from other faiths

Muslims basically believe that Jesus didn't die on the cross but that Allah substituted him for someone who looked like him. Jesus was then taken straight to heaven and the other man was crucified. Most Muslims believe that Allah would never let one of his prophets (they believe Jesus was a prophet) be killed in a dishonourable way like this, so it couldn't possibly have happened.

For children with additional needs

Sometimes children who are wheelchair users will question why they have to put up with being stuck in a chair. There are so many aspects of facing difficulty that cannot be understood in our lives on earth. Everyone has to face different problems and many children have been trusted to cope with very challenging circumstances. God's rescue plan through Jesus gives us hope for a future without fear or pain.

FILE 5

inside wheel to A on the outside wheel). See if the group can then solve this message:

CK GXK YKIXKZ GMKTZY

(We are secret agents)

If you have time, encourage your Agents to come with messages of their own.

ACTIVE AGENTS

45 minutes

Bring everyone together so that the Agents can get active! Play the MISSION:RESCUE theme song as a sign for the children to join the larger group.

Y should come on stage, loaded with ropes and gadgets, and tell the children that X has been kidnapped! He should read out a note he found on X's desk:

Have been taken
Pay £1,000
Help Y

Y explains that X is asking for his help. He asks the children what he needs to go on a rescue, because he doesn't have £1,000 to pay for her release! If they suggest something he already has, he should show it to the children. While the children are shouting out suggestions, X then comes on stage. When Y finally notices her (and the children will probably try to tell him she's there), X explains to the shocked Y that the note was for their assistant, Miss PennyMoney. She had been taken to the dentist and had had to pay £1,000 because the Spy Fitness Instructor knocked four of her teeth out when they were doing keep fit! She was asking Miss PennyMoney to help Y with today's session if she wasn't back in time.

Leave some of Y's rescue equipment on stage next to the sleeping bag, mobile phone and remote control car, and move on with the session.

SPY WORKOUT

The Spy Fitness Instructor (SFI) should lead the workout. Introduce a couple of new activities and invite some volunteers to come and help lead the workout. Everyone needs to be in the best shape to carry out their missions!

SPY SONGS

Reintroduce the CodeCrackers and sing the MISSION: RESCUE theme song, together with the actions. Sing a song that you have already sung at MISSION:RESCUE, and introduce a new one today.

OPERATION: GUNGE RESCUE

Today's special operation is a messy one, so make sure you have plenty of cover-up and clean-up equipment ready. Fill a fairly large container (anything from a large bucket to a baby bath to a paddling or ball pool, depending on space and numbers) with some liquid – either water or, if you're feeling more adventurous, some kind of gooey gunk! (Look for 'Gelli Baff' on the Internet.) Place plastic balls in the liquid (if you're using goo, then make sure some of the balls are beneath the surface). Get three or four Agent volunteers and tell them they have a certain amount of time to 'rescue' the balls from your swamp. The Agent volunteers have to run to the swamp, pull out a ball and then return to the start. You could have more volunteers and run the race like a relay, with each member of the team taking it in turns to retrieve a ball. To make this harder you could use play fishing nets to retrieve the balls. Then, at the end of a given time or when all the balls have been 'rescued' count up the balls and declare a winner!

SECURITY REPORT

The Head of Security comes to deliver today's report. They should make these points:

- Security level snot green.
- X is back from the dentist. It cost £1,000 to sort out her teeth.
- Moses is rescued as a baby, as a young man after killing an Egyptian and by Jethro in the desert.
- Moses meets God and is given everything he needs for the rescue mission.
- Moses and Aaron meet Pharaoh, but he doesn't listen to them.
- Surely God won't let his rescue mission fail because of one setback?

Repeat: security level snot green! Stay alert, Agents!

SPY CHIEF'S CLUES

Introduce the Spy Chief and ask them to reveal their clues for today. The Spy Chief should show his pile of cue cards, but not reveal any apart from the one on top, that should read, 'Hello Chief!' X and Y ask what the pile of cards is for and the Spy Chief explains that they are cards with words to shout out. He shows the top card to the Agents and encourages them to shout back, 'Hello Chief!' He then shows the Agents the next card, 'X has the X Factor!', about which X is very happy. Y should wonder what might be written about him, until the Spy Chief shows the next card, 'But why, Y?!' The Spy Chief explains that the rest of the signs are for today's story.

REVEALING THE SECRET

The Spy Chief should say goodbye to X and Y and go on to tell the story, or introduce today's episode from the MISSION:RESCUE DVD. (If you are telling the story and using the DVD, tell the story with the clues first, then show the DVD.) The Spy Chief should tell the story in their own words or use this script. Before you start, encourage the children to carry on shouting out whenever you hold up a sign:

So what has happened in God's rescue mission so far? God rescued Moses, then appeared to him in the bush that was on fire, but wasn't burning. He gave Moses everything he needed and off Moses went with his brother Aaron to Pharaoh. But do you remember what happened next? Moses and Aaron told Pharaoh that God wanted his people, the Israelites, to leave... (Hold up 'Let my people go!') But Pharaoh said... (Hold up 'No, I won't let your people go!') So Moses was very sad. But God told him that he was in charge, and he would do amazing but terrible things so that Pharaoh would change his mind.

So Moses and Aaron went to Pharaoh and told him that God wanted the Israelites to leave. God turned Aaron's stick into a snake to show Pharaoh how powerful he was, but Pharaoh still said... (Hold up 'No, I won't let your people go!') So Aaron held out his stick over the River Nile and God turned the water to blood. But Pharaoh just turned away.

So, a week later, God told Moses to go back to the king. If he wouldn't listen, God would do something else. He told Aaron to hold out his walking stick again, and when he did, frogs appeared everywhere: in Pharaoh's bed, in the ovens, in the bread mix, crawling everywhere. Pharaoh said... (Hold up 'Your people can go!') And Moses got rid of the frogs. But then Pharaoh changed his mind... (Hold up 'No, I won't let your people go!')

Again and again God sent Moses and Aaron to Pharaoh and Pharaoh refused to listen. So God sent biting gnats and buzzing flies, but Pharaoh still said... (Hold up 'No, I won't let your people go!') God made the pharaoh's cows and sheep very ill, he caused nasty sores to appear on the Egyptians' bodies, but still Pharaoh said... (Hold up 'No, I won't let your people go!') So God made huge hailstones fall from the sky, battering Egypt, and brought enormous clouds of insects called locusts, that ate all the Egyptians plants and food. But Pharaoh said... (Hold up 'No, I won't let your people go!') Then God made it stay dark for three days – people couldn't see anything! But in the end, Pharaoh still said... (Hold up 'No, I won't let your people go!')

And so Moses went to Pharaoh with the last warning. If Pharaoh didn't let the Israelites leave, God would go through the country and kill the eldest child in each Egyptian family. The Israelites had to take a lamb and kill it. Then they had to put some of the lamb's blood above their door. When God saw the blood, he would move on and no one in that house would be hurt. But Pharaoh still said... (Hold up 'No, I won't let your people go!')

Moses was very sad, because he knew that lots of Egyptians would be hurt because the pharaoh wouldn't change his mind. That night, God moved through Egypt and punished Pharaoh terribly, but the Israelites were saved because of the sign around their doors.

Finally, Pharaoh said... (Hold up 'Your people can go!') and this time he meant it. Moses, Aaron and the Israelites were free to leave at last – God's rescue mission had succeeded. But Pharaoh had made his people very sad because he wouldn't listen to God.

CHECKING THE EVIDENCE

Before X and Y return to the stage, have the Spy Chief conclude the storytelling (whether you used the story above or the DVD) with the following:

But God's rescuing wasn't finished yet. For hundreds of years after he had rescued his people from Egypt, they kept ignoring him, just like Pharaoh did. They needed rescuing again: not from being slaves, but from all the wrong things they kept doing. So God put his greatest rescue mission into action: he sent Jesus to live with his people and to give his life for them. Just like the sacrificed lamb saved the Israelites when God moved through Egypt, Jesus would have to die to save God's people (that's everyone, not just the Israelites) from the wrong things they had done. And that means you and me.

X and Y should now return and thank the Spy Chief for the story. They should wonder about some of the things that God did, and say how sad the Egyptians must have been at the end. But God's mission has finally succeeded! After the Chief leaves, X and Y move on to the quiz. Before the session, put together some questions about the story, and also include some that are about the other parts of the morning so far (eg the workout or Operation: gunge rescue). You could include:

- Why did Y think X had been kidnapped? (He found a note on X's desk.)
- What did Pharaoh keep saying to God, Moses and Aaron? ('No, I won't let your people go!')
- What kind of things did God cause to happen? (Accept any of the first nine plagues.)
- What did the Israelites have to do to stay safe? (Kill

FiLE 5

a lamb and put blood above their door.)

- Who is God's ultimate rescuer? (Jesus.)

As always, make the quiz quick and lively, so the children have a chance to review the story and let off some steam after sitting and listening. Use your spy gadget to score the quiz!

TODAY'S MISSION

After the quiz, X and Y should review the day's story, talking through these points:

- Pharaoh didn't listen to Moses and Aaron, even though God kept showing him his power. Moses knew that God was in control.
- God saved the lives of the Israelites, when he was punishing the pharaoh, and his mission succeeded!
- But God had to carry on rescuing his people. And finally, he put his greatest plan into action – he sent Jesus to live with his people. Just like a lamb died to save the Israelites' lives, Jesus had to die to save God's people from all the things they had done wrong.
- Jesus ultimate rescue is still available for us today. If we are sorry for the things we do wrong, and believe that Jesus died to save us, then we can be set free – rescued by God!

THE GODCODE

Tell the children that you are going to talk to God, to pray now. Remind the Agents about the spy prayer action and practise it now. Thank God for being powerful and wanting to save his people, and thank him for sending his son Jesus as his ultimate rescue mission. Give the children a chance to think of something they would like to say to God about today's story, then finish with your 'Amen' shout if you have one.

SPY SONGS

Sing the MISSION:RESCUE theme song again, together with one or two songs that reflect the theme of the day. You could choose:

- 'Anyone can come to God' Reach up! (SU)
- 'Whoopah Wahey' Whoopay Wahey (Kingsway Music)

After the songs, remind everyone about the Interrogation section, where Agents will be able to question a member of the Secret Service. Encourage the Spy Rings to think of questions to ask that SSM. Then send everyone to their spy bases to explore the story more.

GOING UNDERCOVER
45 minutes

THE MAD LABORATORY

Serve your chosen refreshments and chat together about the club so far. What did the children think of today's story? Remind the ring to think of questions for today's interrogation and write them down for Agents X and Y to ask later. Remind them also of the dead-letter drop, where they can leave their jokes and pictures. Go on to explore the Bible passage together more closely.

BIBLE DISCOVERY
With older children

Review the first nine plagues by looking at pages 24 and 25 of Secret Files. Help the children to crack the code to discover the ways God used to free his people. You might want to retell some of the story from Exodus 7–10, but don't dwell too long on this.

Move on to think about the tenth plague. This is a difficult story, so, as you read Exodus 11, help the group think through their responses by writing any thoughts down (in the speech bubbles on pages 26 and 27 or on a separate piece of paper). Spend a few moments discussing the children's thoughts. Acknowledge that this is a difficult story about God, but remind them that Pharaoh wasn't listening to God and was keeping the Israelites as slaves. Think about Exodus 12:29–32 and write any further thoughts in the speech bubble. Encourage the children to be honest with God – to say what they think and ask him the questions that they have.

Think about the Passover, using the retelling on pages 29 and 30, and begin to explore the links to Jesus' sacrifice and God's ultimate rescue mission. There is information you can use on page 31 of Secret Files. To take this further and if you have time, help children explore the idea of Jesus being a rescuer by reading the story of Zacchaeus. (Or show them the pages in their Secret Files and encourage them to complete these at home.) What does it mean that Jesus came to seek out and save the lost? For more information on Jesus being a rescuer, see page 23.

Children may want to make some kind of commitment to follow Jesus today. For more information about helping a child respond to Jesus, see page 24.

With younger children

Think about today's story by ordering the pictures at the top of Spy Sheet 4 (you may need to retell some of the story to remind the children of some of the

details). Explain a little about the Passover meal (see the MISSION:RESCUE website) and then read Exodus 12:24–27. Just like the Israelites said thank you to God for rescuing them, we can say thank you to God for the things he has done for us. Think together about what you might want to say thank you for, and encourage the children to write or draw it in the space provided on the Spy Sheet.

Tell the children about God's final rescue mission. Say how people were still getting things wrong, even after God had rescued them from Egypt. So God had to put his final, best rescue mission into action. He sent Jesus to live with his people and to teach them how to live. Jesus died so that we could be friends with God. Because he died, we could be forgiven for the things we do wrong, and we could be rescued/saved, and have eternal life! Tell something of your own story here, explaining how you yourself were 'rescued'.

With all age groups

Adapt these questions to suit your group, sharing your own feelings, opinions and experiences as appropriate:
- God's rescue mission finally succeeded. What do you think Moses thought about what happened?
- What does this story tell you about God?
- Jesus' mission was to find and save people who are lost because of the wrong things that they do. What about the wrong things that you do? Do you feel like you need rescuing? Do you want to know more about that?

Q-TECH'S WORKSHOP

Choose a construction activity from Q-Tech's spy store (see page 27), deciding whether to do an individual or an all-together construction. For extra ideas, see Ultimate Craft (SU, 978 1 84427 364 5).

SPIES' TIME OUT

Help the Agents let off steam by choosing suitable games from Q-Tech's spy store (see page 27). See page 10 for more info about choosing the best games for your club. For extra games ideas, check out Ultimate Games (SU, 978 1 84427 365 2).

AGENTS ARE GO!

25 minutes

DEAD LETTER DROP

Welcome everyone back together by playing the MISSION:RESCUE theme song. Read out some of the secret messages and pictures from the dead letter drop. Thank all the contributing Agents and remind

everyone that tomorrow is the last chance to put items into the dead letter drop.

SPY SONGS

The CodeCrackers lead a song that you have already sung to start this all-together section.

RETURN OF THE SPY CHIEF

Welcome back the Spy Chief, who goes on to round up what the Spy Rings have been exploring together. The Spy Chief should sum up these points:
- God rescued the Israelites from Egypt, and showed the Israelites and Pharaoh how powerful he is. The rescue mission was a success!
- But God had to carry on rescuing his people. His final rescue plan was to send Jesus to live with his people. Just like a lamb died to save the Israelites' lives, Jesus had to die to save God's people from all the things they had done wrong.
- Jesus' ultimate rescue is still available for us today. Jesus can rescue us! If you want to know more about that, then ask your Spymaster.

INTERROGATION

Introduce the Secret Service member who is to be interrogated. Before the session, go through with the SSM what you're going to talk about – about what being rescued by Jesus means to them, a little about their personal faith story/journey – making sure that their story is appropriate. Interrogate the SSM, including some of the questions the children have thought of. When you have finished, thank the SSM for being willing to be interrogated!

DRAMA: WHO'S THE MOLE?

Introduce the next episode of the drama: 'Who's the mole?' Today the mole is unmasked, and the team achieve their mission's objectives at the last minute! The team are shocked when they find out who the mole is, but they think that everything is now finished. Or is it?

CRACKING THE CODE

With the help of the CodeCrackers, carry on learning the Learn and remember verse for MISSION:RESCUE, Psalm 118:24, by singing the Learn and remember verse song.

If you're not using the song, ask each Spy Ring to come up with some actions or signs for the words of the verse, then ask some of the Spy Rings to 'perform' their actions as you all say the verse together. If you have time, you could take signs from different groups and make a version that the whole club can do together.

COMPLETING THE MISSION

Round off Agents are go! by asking the children what they have enjoyed at MISSION:RESCUE today and then include those things in a short prayer of thanks, using your spy prayer action (and shout). Sing the MISSION: RESCUE theme song and send the Agents back to their Spy Rings to round off the day's session.

AGENTS' DEBRIEF

10 minutes

As you sit together for the final time today, chat about the highlights of the day. Finish any pages of Secret Files or sections of the Spy Sheets you have not done, or carry on with the construction or activity from Agents' briefing. Alternatively, pray together using this prayer activity:

CHAT WITH GOD

What you need

☐ Flatbread (pitta bread is ideal, or crackers)
☐ Plates or serviettes

What you do

Remind the children about the Passover meal, the meal that God told the Israelites to eat to celebrate God's rescue mission. God's people ate the lamb with flat bread, and they remembered what God had done for them. Share the flatbread or crackers around and, as you eat them, ask the children what they'd like to remember and celebrate about what God has done for them. It might be as recent as something they have experienced at MISSION:RESCUE or something else about their walk with God. Have a suggestion of your own ready to help the children think. Once everyone has shared (who wants to share), then mention all these things in a prayer.

(Before you do this activity, be aware of the allergy issues involving your group.)

As the children are picked up from their Spy Rings, make sure they are reminded of the next session, and that they take all of their belongings with them. Make sure too that they remember to bring in jokes, pictures and questions for the dead letter drop. Each Spymaster should know how each of the children in their group is getting home.

MISSION CLEAR UP

30 minutes

After all the children have gone, clear up from the day's events and set up for the next session. Meet together as a team to debrief. Continue to feed back what is working and what might need tweaking. Have a brief time of prayer where everyone together prays for the whole club, thanking God for what he has done so far and lifting up any concerns to him. If you have the time and the facilities, you may wish to share a meal together.

SPY SHEET 4
Mission accomplished

TOP SECRET

Can you remember what happens in today's story? Listen as your Spymaster retells the story and then put these pictures in the right order.

God's mission was complete! And Moses told God's people, the Israelites, to tell their children and their grandchildren about how God rescued them.

Has God done anything good for you? It might be bringing you to MISSION: RESCUE! Write or draw it here, then tell your Spy Ring about it!

Ask your Spymaster about God's final rescue mission – Jesus!

MISSION 5
Escape!

Mission briefing

SPIRITUAL PREPARATION

READ TOGETHER

Read Exodus 13:17–22 together and wonder at what this huge crowd of people must have looked like, being led by a pillar of cloud by day and fire by night. Then go on to read Exodus 14:1–29. Ask someone who is good at storytelling to read this out to the group expressively, so that you can get some impression of the pace of the story.

EXPLORE TOGETHER

In pairs or threes, consider the emotions of the Israelites as they experience the chase – from the joy of leaving Egypt to the astonishment at God's victory. Then reflect on these questions:

- Why does God harden Pharaoh's heart one final time?
- What do you think of God's question to Moses in verse 15: 'Why do you keep calling out to me for help?'
- If you were in Moses' place, what would you think of this final confrontation?

When all the groups have finished, gather back together and feed back the thoughts of each group.

REFLECT TOGETHER

This final act of rescue in the Israelites' liberation from Egypt is no less dramatic than the ones before, but here we see such an awesome and unlikely demonstration of God's power – to stop water in its tracks and create a pathway through the water. There is no doubt that the God we follow is an amazing one, the most powerful and the most just.

But God set this up; he sent the Israelites to the edge of the sea so that the Egyptians would chase them. In the excitement of the story, the children will probably not pick this up, but it's worth

KEY PASSAGE
Exodus 14:1–29

KEY AIMS
- to be amazed at how powerful God is and at what he can do, and to respond appropriately
- to provide a fun final day of the programme for children and to encourage them to return to the Sunday service (if you're having one) and other future events

KEY STORY
God rescues the Israelites from the chasing Egyptians by miraculously parting the Red Sea. When there was no way out that the Israelites could see, God provided one, using Moses as the instrument for this final rescue of the story. God's people are free!

For children with no church background
This is an exciting adventure story that matches anything that children will read or see on TV. Use the excitement of the story to encourage children with little or no church background to wonder at how God protected his people from danger. Help them explore the idea that God continues to rescue – heading towards his ultimate rescue plan of Jesus.

For church children
This is another story that church children may well be familiar with, but placing it in its context, coming after God has rescued Israel from the Egyptians and Pharaoh will help them understand more about God's rescuing power. Saving them from slavery was only a part – he rescued them from certain death too. Go on to link the story of Jesus with Moses' story. This was explored yesterday, but today's story should help children place Moses and Jesus in God's overarching story of salvation.

For children from other faiths
God rescuing us is one of the points where Christianity significantly differs from all other faiths. We are saved by his grace not by our works. You might need to explain this very carefully to help children of other faiths understand what could be a significant shift in perception.

For children with additional needs
Nothing is impossible for God. The story lends itself to using all the senses to explore it. Don't underestimate what God is doing.

'A smile during a song for the first time may be a step of faith. Touching someone's arm quite deliberately during prayers may be an important response to God's love. A scribbled picture of Jesus may give a whole new expression to someone's spirituality. These small responses are as valid as reciting a creed for someone for whom doctrine is difficult to comprehend.'
Lowe, A, **Evangelism and Learning Disability**, Grove (1998)

spending a moment reflecting on why this miraculous escape happens: to bring glory to God and to make the Egyptians realise that he is God.

What things in your life bring glory to God? How can people in general, and the children at MISSION:RESCUE, in particular, see the power and glory of God in your life?

PRAY TOGETHER
- Pray for the children that have been with you at MISSION:RESCUE. Remember them each by name and thank God for their coming this week.
- Pray for the events you have planned today.
- Pray that God would show his glory to the children today.
- Pray for the friendships built during the club that they would continue in some way.
- Pray for each other, that God will give you everything you need as you work for him.

PRACTICAL PREPARATION

Talk through your programme together, ensuring that everyone knows their part in the day and has everything they need. Set up the different areas of the club and make sure that everything is in place. Make sure you make any adjustments you agreed in your evaluation session after the previous session. Even on this last 'club' day, encourage the team to continue welcoming the children (and their families if possible).

WHAT YOU NEED CHECKLIST
- ☐ **Registration** Registration forms, badges, labels, pens, team lists
- ☐ **Spy Rings** Bibles, Secret Files or Spy Sheets, Bible discovery notes, pens and pencils
- ☐ **Music** The CodeCrackers band or backing tracks
- ☐ **Drama** Costume and props
- ☐ **Q-Tech** PA system, laptop, PowerPoints and projection/OHP and acetates, MISSION:RESCUE DVD
- ☐ **Activities** Equipment for games and construction
- ☐ **Agents X and Y** Running order, notes, quiz questions, Operation: capture equipment
- ☐ **The mad laboratory** Drinks and biscuits, or other refreshments
- ☐ **Spy Chief** Story script, props for the story

On the mission

As the children arrive and register, play some spy-themed music (such as Bond or Mission Impossible theme tunes) and display the MISSION:RESCUE logo on the screen to welcome the children.

Have plenty of the team available in the registration area to welcome any new children, to chat to parents and to make sure everyone knows where they are going. Spymasters and Assistants should be ready in their bases to welcome and chat with their Agents.

AGENTS' BRIEFING
10 minutes

As the children arrive, if you started the spy base activity in the first session, put the finishing touches to your base. Otherwise try this activity.

SPY LANGUAGE
What you need
- ☐ Pens and paper (optional)

What you do
Work together to create code words for some of the things you see at MISSION:RESCUE. These might include the room where you meet, your own spy base area, refreshments, even the pens or pencils you use in the Spy Ring. Compile a list of these code words and see if you can communicate using some of the ideas you have come up with. Here are some suggestions:
- **The room where you meet**: spy central, secret bunker, the lair
- **Your spy base**: safe house, the eagle's nest (or a code word related to the name of your group or where your group is situated)
- **Pens/pencils**: message sticks, inscribers
- **Refreshments**: spy rations, life stuff, belly blessings

Join together with another Spy Ring and see if they can work out what your code words mean from listening to you speak!

ACTIVE AGENTS
45 minutes

Bring everyone together so that the Agents can get active! Play the MISSION:RESCUE theme song as a sign for the children to join the larger group.

X and Y welcome the children and tell them that they have to make sure that their escape routes are all set and ready – you never know as a spy when you'll have to make a quick exit. X describes to Y her escape plan, which should be fairly sensible, using fire exits or easily accessible doors. Y then goes off stage and returns with a pile of complicated-looking equipment (use anything outdoors-y that you can get – ropes, karabiners, harnesses, an ice axe, crampons!). He then describes a completely outlandish escape involving jumping out of windows, abseiling down buildings, running through crowded streets, leaping over walls etc.

X should ask the children which of the rescue plans is the best one. She should insist that hers is the best, as it's the safest and most sensible. Y should say that his is more fun. Let the children decide which one they think is best! When the children have made their choice, put some of Y's equipment next to the other props from previous days (make sure it's different from what was left from Day 4). Then go on with the programme.

SPY WORKOUT

The Spy Fitness Instructor (SFI) should lead the workout. Introduce a couple of new activities and invite some volunteers to come and help lead the workout. Comment that today you're going to be doing something amazing, and that you'll need to be in the best shape!

SPY SONGS

Reintroduce the CodeCrackers and sing the MISSION: RESCUE theme song, together with the actions. Sing a couple of songs that you have already sung at MISSION:RESCUE.

OPERATION: CAPTURE

Today's special operation is all about trying to catch something – it's the old fairground game 'catch the rat'. This can be put together with a long piece of tubing (such as drainpipe), fixed vertically to a board, leaving a gap at the bottom. First, buy a toy stuffed rat or make one using old socks or tights stuffed with pieces of fabric or paper. Knot the end of the socks or tights to make the body, cutting the remaining length into three strips and plaiting tightly to make a tail. As you drop your rat down the tube, the player has to whack it with a rolled up newspaper. It's harder than it looks! Get a volunteer from each of the Spy Rings to compete in the catch the rat challenge. Encourage the Agents to cheer for their volunteer. If the children turn out to be good at this, play until all but one of them has missed the rat. If they're not, then play until someone manages to hit the rat! Award points if you are using them.

SECURITY REPORT

The Head of Security comes to deliver today's report. They should make these points:
- Security level Tardis blue.
- X/Y voted the best escaper (whoever won the children's vote).
- Moses is rescued as a baby, as a young man after killing an Egyptian and by Jethro in the desert.
- Moses meets God and is given everything he needs for the rescue mission.

- Moses and Aaron meet Pharaoh, but he doesn't listen to them.
- God rescues the Israelites from Egypt by showing his power ten times to Pharaoh.
- We are getting reports from our contacts that God's people are in trouble. They need an escape plan!
Repeat: security level Tardis blue! Stay alert, Agents!

SPY CHIEF'S CLUES

Introduce the Spy Chief and ask them to reveal their clues for today. The Spy Chief should produce long strips of blue fabric, a large walking stick, an illustration of the chasing Egyptians, cut out and mounted on a stick, and some (empty) suitcases and bags. The Chief makes a big thing of struggling to bring everything on stage, asking X and Y for help. X and Y should try to work out what the clues all mean. X could make a flag out of some of the blue fabric and the stick, Y could get tangled up in the rest of the blue material as he tries to work out what it is. The Chief reminds the children that they have seen the stick before – it's the stick that turned into a snake! The Chief then unwinds Y and retrieves the clues from X and says that all will become clear when he tells the story.

REVEALING THE SECRET

The Spy Chief should say goodbye to X and Y and go on to tell the story, or introduce today's episode from the MISSION:RESCUE DVD. (If you are telling the story and using the DVD, tell the story with the clues first, then show the DVD.) The Spy Chief should tell the story in their own words or use this script. Introduce some sound effects the children should make during the story when they hear certain words:
- Walk, walking – 'Phew!'
- Chase, chasing – make a galloping noise by tapping hands on thighs
- Water – 'Splish! Splash!'
- Scared – 'Argh!'

So Pharaoh had finally let God's people go – God's rescue mission had succeeded. But there was still one bit of rescuing to do. And this was going to be spectacular! But Moses had to trust God, and that wasn't going to be easy.

When Pharaoh realised that God's people were walking (Sound effect.) out of Egypt, he changed his mind… again. Even after all that God had done! So he decided that he was going to chase (Sound effect.) after them. Pharaoh got everything ready that he needed for the chase (Sound effect.) – he took 600 chariots! (Show the illustration of the chasing Egyptians.) And off he set chasing (Sound effect.) after the Israelites.

The Israelites had been walking (**Sound effect.**) for a long time and were tired (**Ask for some volunteers to come forward and be the Israelites. Give them the baggage to carry.**), when they came to the very edge of some water. (**Sound effect.**) They had arrived at the Red Sea. It was large, and there was no way across the water (**Sound effect.**) – no bridge, no ferry, nothing. (**Spread the blue cloth among the children listening, and encourage them to waft the fabric up and down to make waves. Make sure you leave a gap down the middle for the 'sea' to be parted later.**)

Then the Israelites noticed that the Egyptians were chasing (**Sound effect.**) them. (**Move the Egyptians closer to the 'Israelites'.**) The Israelites were scared (**Sound effect.**) and complained to God and Moses – why had God led them here? They were really scared! (**Sound effect.**) But Moses said to the people, 'Don't be afraid! God will save you; he will save you today. God will fight for you!'

Then God told Moses to hold out his stick over the sea so that it would part and they could cross over on dry land. And so that's what Moses did. He held out his stick over the sea and God used a strong wind to make the water (**Sound effect.**) part right down the middle! (**Hold out the stick over the children and encourage the children in the middle of the group to shuffle sideways so that you get a pathway through the group.**)

The Israelites were still scared (**Sound effect.**) but Moses told them to walk (**Sound effect.**) through the middle of the sea. They set off. They were still scared (**Sound effect.**), but they all walked (**Sound effect.**) in between the giant walls of water. (**Sound effect.**) They knew the Egyptians were still chasing (**Sound effect.**) them (**Move the Egyptians to the start of the pathway through the children.**), so they started walking (**Sound effect.**) more quickly. Eventually they all got to the other side. They had walked (**Sound effect.**) safely across the sea! God certainly was amazing! He was powerful enough to separate one side of the water (**Sound effect.**) from the other! Wow!

When everyone had walked (**Sound effect.**) across, God told Moses to hold the stick over the water (**Sound effect.**) again. The water closed up and the Israelites were safe. God had rescued them again!

Depending on your group, you can tell how the Egyptians were swallowed up by the water when Moses held out his stick at the end. However, this may not be appropriate if you have lots of younger children in the club.

CHECKING THE EVIDENCE

X and Y should return to the stage and thank the Spy Chief for such an amazing story. Congratulate the children for doing so well with the actions and sound effects, and give the 'Israelites' a round of applause as they sit down. All three should continue to be amazed at how God saved the Israelites this time. Count together how many rescues God has made this week (Moses from death, Moses from the river, Moses after killing the Egyptian, the Israelites from Egypt and the Israelites from the chasing Egyptians). After the Chief leaves, X and Y move on to the quiz. Before the session, put together some questions about the story, and also include some that are about the other parts of the morning so far (eg the workout or Operation: capture). You could include:

- Who was voted the best escaper? (X or Y, whoever the children chose.)
- How many chariots did the Pharaoh have? (600.)
- What did Moses hold over the sea? (His stick/staff.)
- What did God use to part the water? (A wind.)

As always, make the quiz quick and lively, so the children have a chance to review the story and let off some steam after sitting and listening.

TODAY'S MISSION

After the quiz, X and Y should review the day's story, talking through these points:

- There's no limit to God's rescuing ability! Even though God had rescued Moses and the Israelites many times already, he was still looking after them.
- God is powerful – he was able to save the Israelites from the big and strong Egyptian army chasing them. But he was powerful enough to separate a path in the sea, so that the Israelites could cross. That's amazingly powerful!

We learnt about Jesus in Mission 4, about how he is God's ultimate rescuer. Just as God never stopped rescuing the Egyptians when they needed it, God sent Jesus to save us – there's no limit to his rescuing ability. That's what the name 'Jesus' means: God saves! It's never too late to be saved by Jesus – we can ask him any time!

THE GODCODE

Tell the children that you are going to talk to God, to pray now. Remind the Agents about the spy prayer action and practise it now. Thank God for being amazing and powerful enough to save his people again and again. Thank God too for Jesus, and ask him to help us find out more about Jesus' rescue mission. Give the children a chance to think of something they would like to say to God about today's story, then finish with your 'Amen' shout if you have one.

SPY SONGS

Sing the MISSION:RESCUE theme song again, together with one or two songs that reflect the theme of the day. You could choose:

- 'How did Moses cross the Red Sea?' kidsource (Kevin Mayhew Ltd)
- 'So amazing God' Light for Everyone (SU)

After the songs, introduce the Interrogation section, where Agents will be able to question a member of the Secret Service. Encourage the Spy Rings to think of questions to ask that SSM. Then send everyone to their spy bases to explore the story more.

GOING UNDERCOVER

45 minutes

THE MAD LABORATORY

Serve your chosen refreshments and chat together about the club so far. What did the children think of today's story? Remind the Ring to think of questions for today's interrogation and write them down for Agents X and Y to ask later. Remind them also of the dead letter drop, where they can leave their jokes and pictures. Go on to explore the Bible passage together more closely.

BIBLE DISCOVERY

With older children

On page 35 of Secret Files, encourage the children to match up what they think each person or thing can lift. Which is the most powerful? You could chat together about what superpower each of the Agents might have if they were a superhero, if you think the children would be interested. Go on to think about what powerful thing they heard about in today's story.

Read Exodus 14 together (using a Bible or Secret Files pages 36–39), stopping at verses 9, 12, 14, 23, 25 and 29 to decide how the Israelites were feeling. What was it like to be part of what was happening? As you read, you could act out the story (as you did in Active Agents), with the children as the Israelites, stopping to think about the emotions involved. On page 39, can the Agents spot the differences in the two pictures?

Go on to use the questions on page 41 to reflect on the story and how powerful the Agents think God is. Let the Agents put a mark on the line where they think it should go. Make sure they know that this is a personal response and they don't need to worry about what other people have put.

Before the session, with your Assistant, chat together about what you might say to your Spy Ring about how amazing and powerful you think Jesus is. If you have any personal experiences that the Agents might find amazing, you could tell them here. When you have finished, give the group time to write a couple of things from what you said about Jesus that they find interesting.

Finally, ask the group to think about their response to Jesus. In their own time, and again not worrying about what others are doing, encourage them to circle the statement that they think is closest to the way they feel on page 42. If any of the Agents want to chat to you, find space to do so. If any of the children want to know more about becoming a Christian, you could use page 43. There is more information on leading a child to Christ on page 24.

With younger children

Using Spy Sheet 5, ask the children for some suggestions of powerful things or people. Get them to choose one of the pictures on Spy Sheet 5 that they think is the most powerful. They may not all choose the same one! If you like, everyone could think about what superpower they might have if they were a superhero!

Go on to either read Exodus 14 (using the CEV or similar translation), or retell it in your own words. If you're using the Bible text, read verses 1–9 and pause, letting the children draw where the two groups of people are. (They can use stick people, dots or whatever they're comfortable drawing.) Then read verses 10–16, 21 and 22 and pause again, giving time to draw. Finally read verses 23–28 and encourage the group to draw the Israelites safe on the far side. (Be sensitive to your group, if your Spy Ring is particularly young, as the end of this story means that all the Egyptians and their horses die.) If you're retelling the story in your own words, make sure you pause at the appropriate points (listed above) so the Agents can mark on their map where everyone is at that particular point.

As this is the last time your Spy Ring will be exploring the Bible together at MISSION:RESCUE, let the children write down what they have found out about God and what they think in the speech bubble at the bottom of the Spy Sheet. Chat with any of your Agents who would like to.

With all age groups

Adapt these questions to suit your group, sharing your own feelings, opinions and experiences as appropriate:

- What would you have thought if you were one of the Israelites and were trapped next to the sea?

- What would you have thought if you were one of the Israelites and you saw a pathway open up in the sea?
- What do you think this story tells you about God?
- What do you want to say to God after hearing and thinking about this story?

Q-TECH'S WORKSHOP

Choose a construction activity from Q-Tech's spy store (see page 27), deciding whether to do an individual or an all-together construction. For extra ideas, see Ultimate Craft (SU, 978 1 84427 364 5)

SPIES' TIME OUT

Help the Agents let off steam by choosing suitable games from Q-Tech's spy store (see page 27). See page 10 for more information about choosing the best games for your club. For extra games ideas, check out Ultimate Games (SU, 978 1 84427 365 2).

AGENTS ARE GO!

25 minutes

DEAD LETTER DROP

Welcome everyone back together by playing the MISSION:RESCUE theme song. Read out some of the secret messages and pictures from the dead-letter drop. Thank all the contributing Agents for putting their secret messages, codes, jokes and pictures in the dead letter drop this week.

SPY SONGS

The CodeCrackers lead a song that you have already sung to start this all-together section.

RETURN OF THE SPY CHIEF

Welcome back the Spy Chief, who goes on to round up what the Spy Rings have been exploring together. The Spy Chief should sum up these points:

- Today we have seen how powerful and amazing God is. He never stops rescuing his people.
- God sent Jesus to rescue all people – this rescue mission is for us.
- If we want to be rescued, then we can talk to Jesus about it. If anyone would like to know more about that, then they should talk to their Spymaster or Assistant.
- All through MISSION:RESCUE, we have seen how God loves his people so much, and that he is powerful enough to rescue them from anything – pharaohs, armies, even the things we do wrong. Wow – God is totally amazing!

INTERROGATION

Introduce the Secret Service member who is to be interrogated. Before the session, go through with the SSM what you're going to talk about – again today, you can discuss what being rescued by Jesus means to the SSM, giving a little of their personal story – making sure that their story is appropriate. Interrogate the SSM, including some of the questions the children have thought of. When you have finished, thank the SSM for being willing to be interrogated!

DRAMA: WHO'S THE MOLE?

Introduce the next episode of the drama: 'The final escape'. Even though the team know who the mole is, they are still in danger. The mole comes after them and they need to escape – will they get away?

CRACKING THE CODE

With the help of the CodeCrackers, sing the Learn and remember verse song. Can the children sing the song without any help from the SSMs or CodeCrackers?

If you're not using the song, work together in Spy Rings to write the words of the verse on different pieces of paper (one word per piece). Each Spy Ring should use a different coloured paper. The Agents then hide these sheets of paper around the room. Assign each Spy Ring a different colour from the one they used and challenge them to find all the words of that colour and put the verse in the right order. When everyone has finished, say the verse together.

COMPLETING THE MISSION

Round off Agents are go! by asking the children what they have enjoyed at MISSION:RESCUE today and at the whole club and then include those thingd in a short prayer of thanks, using your spy prayer action (and shout). Thank all the Agents for being part of MISSION: RESCUE and remind them of the MISSION:RESCUE debrief (Sunday service), if you are having one. Sing the MISSION:RESCUE theme song and send the Agents back to their Spy Rings to round off the day's session.

AGENTS' DEBRIEF

10 minutes

As you sit together for the final time today, chat about the highlights of the day and the club as a whole. Finish any pages of Secret Files or sections of the Spy Sheets you have not done, or carry on with the construction or activity from Agents' briefing. Alternatively, pray together using this prayer activity:

CHAT WITH GOD

What you do

As this is the last time that your Spy Ring will be meeting together, use this time to pray for each other. Organise the children so that you are all standing in a circle. Ask them to turn to their left and put their hand on the shoulder of the person in front. Encourage the Agents to pray for that person, asking God to be with them as they leave MISSION:RESCUE. Then turn around and do the same for the person on the other side. If your group is confident, encourage them to pray out loud all at the same time. If not, say that they can pray silently for each other.

As the children are picked up from their Spy Rings, make sure they are reminded of the MISSION:RESCUE debrief (Sunday service), if you're having one. If not, let them know of the activities you are running to follow up the club (midweek clubs, activity days, Sunday groups etc), so that they have the chance to carry on in their relationship with God's people! Ensure that they take all of their belongings with them too. Each Spymaster should know how each of the children in their group is getting home.

MISSION CLEAR UP

30 minutes

After all the children have gone, clear up from the day's events. You may need to have an extended clear up session, if you are not using your venue again. Meet together as a team to debrief and make sure everyone knows the plan for the Sunday service, if you are having one. Have a brief time of prayer where everyone together prays for the whole club, thanking God for what he has done and lifting up all the children. If you have the time and the facilities, you may wish to share a meal together.

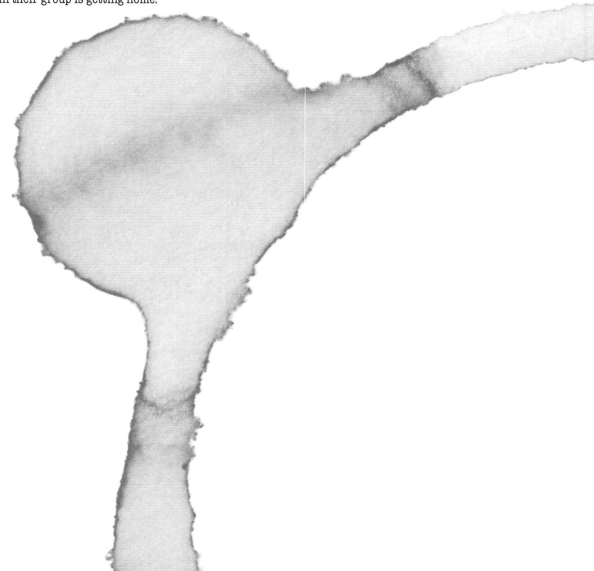

SPY SHEET 5
Escape!

What is the most powerful thing you can think of?
Circle the picture you think is the most powerful!

Listen to your Spymaster telling the
story and follow the action on the map
below! When your Spymaster stops, draw
where the Israelites and Egyptians are.

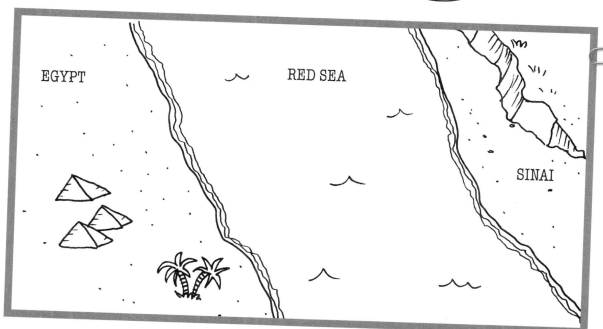

EGYPT

RED SEA

SINAI

God rescued the Israelites again!
How powerful do you think God is?
More powerful than a weightlifter?
More powerful than a crane?

What do you want to say to God?

MISSION END

SUNDAY SERVICE 2

Debrief

KEY PASSAGE
Exodus 15:1-18

KEY AIMS
- to give thanks to God for all he has done, and to look forward to God's plans in the future
- to celebrate MISSION:RESCUE

KEY STORY
Moses and the Israelites celebrate their rescue by God and the success of his mission. We too can celebrate! We can thank God for the MISSION:RESCUE club and all we have learned. We can look forward, too, to our continuing relationship with him and our part in his plans.

This service rounds off the club, but don't let it be the last time you have contact with the children from your club (and their families). Use this time to celebrate what God has done (in the club, for the Israelites and for us through Jesus), and also to let people know the activities of your church and what they can come along to/get involved with. Remember that this should not be about the children 'performing' elements of the club for their families and the church congregation. This is a time for the club and the church family to worship and celebrate together.

For children with no church background
You may well have many children and families in your congregation who have never attended church before, so make sure they feel welcome. As you prepare your service, keep these people in mind, and ensure you don't use jargon, and that the songs you sing are not too confessional (so you don't ask people to sing things they don't believe). This service is all about celebration and all children can engage with this idea – make the most of this link!

For church children
Children and families from a church background are going to be used to being in church, but make sure that they are welcoming to people from outside the church family. Help them to celebrate inclusively. The idea of celebrating what God has done is familiar to these children, but don't let it become 'samey'; make this a new and exciting celebration!

For children from other faiths
When you encourage children to bring their parents to this service, always talk about inviting families. If the children come from Asian or Middle Eastern backgrounds it is more common to think about families rather than just parents. And be ready – if things go well you will get very large families coming!.

For children with additional needs
Make this a time to celebrate – use flags, streamers or shakers if a child has no voice and be ready with ear defenders and clear schedules for any children on the autistic spectrum.

Think about the family situations. Now that you have a good relationship with the child, how can you, as a church or as an individual, support the family in the future – babysitting, meals, washing, shopping or being a befriender in a regular church children's group?

PRACTICAL PREPARATIONS
- [ ] **Music** The CodeCrackers band or backing tracks
- [ ] **Drama** Costume and props
- [ ] **Q-Tech** PA system, laptop, PowerPoints and projection/OHP and acetates
- [ ] **Agents X and Y** Running order, notes
- [ ] **The mad laboratory** a range of refreshments for after the service
- [ ] **Spy Chief** Story script

On the mission

OPENING AND WELCOME
As Sunday service 1, the church leader (N) should welcome everyone to the church and service. They should introduce Agents X and Y and invite them to give a few highlights of the club. X and Y should have one or two 'headlines' to tell the congregation of what has been happening in the club. Include some comments about God completing his mission to rescue his people.

SPY SONGS

Sing two or three songs that you have been singing at MISSION:RESCUE, including the MISSION:RESCUE song. If you have been using action songs, then get some volunteer Agents to help with the actions! In all your music for this service, you'll need to strike a balance between children and adults, and church and non-church people. Try to be as inclusive as you can.

OPERATION: BALLOON RESCUE

Before the session, blow up lots of balloons, enough to fill a paddling pool. Put all the balloons into the paddling pool, together with some party items, such as party hats, party poppers or party blowers. Explain that all week you have been having Agent-training activities called Operations and that this is called Operation: Balloon rescue. Invite some volunteers to come up and give them 30 seconds to find as many party related items in the balloon pool as they can. At the end of 30 seconds, count up the party items and declare a winner. You could have a prize (or they could keep the party items they have found!).

SECURITY REPORT

Invite the Head of Security to give today's security report:

- Security level shining gold!
- Moses is rescued as a baby, as a young man after killing an Egyptian and by Jethro in the desert.
- Moses meets God and is given everything he needs for the rescue mission.
- Moses and Aaron meet Pharaoh, but he doesn't listen to them.
- God rescues the Israelites from Egypt by showing his power ten times to Pharaoh. God rescues the Israelites from the Egyptian army by parting the Red Sea so that they can escape!

Repeat: security level shining gold! Enjoy the celebrations, Agents!

PRAYER

Lead everyone in a prayer (making sure you explain carefully what you're doing) thanking God for bringing everyone here today, and thanking him for all you have learnt at MISSION:RESCUE.

HEARING THE MESSAGE

Ask an SSM to read Exodus 15:1–18.

SPY CHIEF'S CLUES

The Spy Chief comes on with one of the props from each of the stories you have explored at MISSION:RESCUE:

- **Mission start**: Lego® bricks
- **Mission 1**: Moses basket
- **Mission 2**: Fire (either the film footage, or a picture of a fire)
- **Mission 3**: Aaron's secret message
- **Mission 4**: 'No, I won't let your people go!' sign
- **Mission 5**: the Egyptian army picture

X and Y, and the children, should help the Chief briefly remember what all the clues mean.

REVEALING THE SECRET

The Chief thanks X and Y and goes on to briefly retell the six stories, inviting different Agents to hold the visuals for him as he goes along:

(Holding the Lego® bricks.) The Israelites lived in Egypt, but they were treated really badly. The king, who was called the pharaoh, hated the Israelites and made them work. They had to make bricks and build cities and temples for the pharaoh. They were very unhappy, but God had heard their cries for help and was ready with his rescue mission.

(Holding the Moses basket.) Pharaoh tried to kill all the Israelite baby boys, so that the number of Israelites would stop getting bigger. But Moses' mother put him in a basket and set him adrift on the River Nile. The basket came to rest near where the pharaoh's daughter was having a bath. She saw the basket and baby Moses and decided to bring him up herself. But when Moses got older, he got in serious trouble and had to run away. He went to a place called Midian, where he became a shepherd. God had rescued Moses several times, because Moses was going to be God's rescue agent!

(Holding the picture of fire, or pointing to it on the screen.) Moses was out with his sheep one day when he saw a strange thing – he saw a bush that was on fire, but that wasn't burning up. This was a special fire, and God spoke to him through it. He told Moses to go to Egypt and rescue his people. Moses didn't think he was up to it, but God gave him everything he needed – the words to say, his brother Aaron to say the words and even a walking stick that he could use to do miracles (God even turned it into a snake!). The mission was ready to go!

(Holding the message from Aaron.) But it didn't all go well! Moses and Aaron went to Pharaoh, but he didn't want to let the Israelites go. In fact, the pharaoh was angry and made the Israelites lives' worse. Moses didn't know what to do and complained bitterly to God. But God reminded Moses that he was in control. He was going to rescue the Israelites, because he was powerful – he was God! So Moses and Aaron went back to Pharaoh…

(Holding the sign.) Moses and Aaron kept going back to Pharaoh, but Pharaoh kept saying… (Show the sign and see if anyone shouts out what's written.) So God showed his power through ten signs: blood and frogs, gnats and flies, sick animals and boils, hail and locusts, darkness and… the last sign was the most terrible. Pharaoh was so stubborn that God announced he would kill every firstborn thing in Egypt. Pharaoh wouldn't listen, and that's what happened. Finally Pharaoh agreed to let the Israelites go. The mission was a success! Until…

(Holding the Egyptian army picture.) Pharaoh changed his mind again. When the Israelites had gone, he decided he wanted them back. So he chased after them with his army in 600 chariots! When he caught up with them, the Israelites were at the edge of the Red Sea, with no sign of escape. But God opened up a pathway through the sea and the Israelites crossed to safety. God closed the pathway and the Egyptians were trapped in the sea – they were defeated for good. The Israelites were safe and this part of God's rescue mission was complete.

CHECKING THE EVIDENCE

X and Y thank the Chief and then introduce the quiz and the spy scoring gadget (here you could award numbers of sweets instead of points). Review the six stories by asking some quiz questions, as well as questions about the club itself. You could try:

- What were the Israelites forced to do by Pharaoh? (Make bricks and build.)
- Who found Moses in the river? (Pharaoh's daughter.)
- What was strange about the bush Moses saw? (It was on fire, but wasn't burning up.)
- What did Moses do when Pharaoh refused to let the people go? (He complained to God.)
- How many signs did God perform to convince Pharaoh? (Ten.)
- How did God help the Israelites to escape the army? (He made a pathway through the sea.)

Congratulate everyone on doing so well!

SPY SONGS

Include a couple of songs here, again being careful about the songs that you choose. Go to the MISSION: RESCUE website for some ideas.

REVEALING THE SECRET

X and Y then go on to talk about these teaching points:

- Moses' song that we heard earlier was a celebration of what God had done. God had rescued Moses and the Israelites so many times that Moses just had to sing praises to God to say thank you.

- But God hasn't stopped rescuing people. He sent Jesus to rescue people from the wrong things that they do. He was killed, even though he hadn't done anything wrong. He took the punishment for what we had done. And so we are saved if we believe in him. This rescue is open to everyone.
- So at MISSION:RESCUE we have heard many amazing things that God has done that we should say thanks for!

THE GODCODE

Remind the children of their prayer action and shout, although this time you're going to do something different. There are two choices of how to pray (or you could do both!). If you think you'll have an active congregation, then give out the balloons from Operation: balloon rescue and some marker pens. Ask people to write things on the balloons that they want to thank God for. When everyone has finished, play some music and encourage the congregation to tap the balloons to each other, while shouting out thanks for whatever is written on the balloons. For a more reflective prayer time, give out sticky notes and pens, and ask people to write their thanks on a sticky note. Play some music and ask people to come to the front and stick their stickies to a large sheet of paper. As they do so, they should thank God for the thing they have written down.

At the end of the prayer time, do your prayer action or shout again.

SPY SONGS

Sing the MISSION:RESCUE song again to finish the service. Make sure everyone knows about the appropriate events in your church's programme, that they can come along to next.

AFTER THE SERVICE

After the service has finished, make sure all new children and families are welcomed. It might be an idea to have another family lunch event, maybe involving Passover or spy-themed food. What you can do is dictated by the skills you have on your team, your facilities and the situation you're running your club in, but see if there's anything that will fit all these considerations.

Continuing the mission

Follow-up ideas

During your holiday club week, you will more than likely make contact with children and families who have little or no regular connection with church. At MISSION: RESCUE the children will have heard truths from the gospel, built positive relationships with your team and enjoyed being in community. It's a long time to wait until you do it all again next year! The following ideas aim to enable you to continue the important work you have begun and begin to disciple the children on a more regular basis, turning your holiday club ministry into a year-round ministry to children who may be currently outside the reach of your church.

FAMILY MINISTRY

It is vital to remember that children are part of families and that mission to the whole family is an essential part of passing on the stories and love of Jesus.

With a view to reaching the whole family, start inviting them to belong to the community, through events and in developing relationships. Once good relationships have been established, personal faith might be shared. This might take a long time to develop, but long-term commitment to children and families is essential. The ideas here will provide you with some starting points for continuing the work with the children and for connecting with whole families.

Top Tips on Growing faith with families
SU, 978 1 84427 249 5 £3.50 is full of helpful advice if you're looking to start a family ministry.

AFTERNOON/EVENING ACTIVITIES

The MISSION:RESCUE daily outlines provide enough material for one session: morning or afternoon. However, depending on the energy levels of your team and financial resources of your children/families/church, the holiday club lends itself to an optional extended programme, which could involve having a 'Spy school' room or event full of techie ideas, digital cameras, Scalextric, Spy Kids DVDs (with appropriate licence), Google earth and satellite views, and Hubble and NASA links. You could run games and/or construction afternoons, using some of the more popular choices in MISSION:RESCUE, together with options you didn't have time to try out during the club. You could even have some kind of secret agent competition!

Events like these can be used to extend the MISSION: RESCUE theme over the whole summer holidays, with afternoon or evening events taking place in the weeks following the club.

FAMILY REUNION EVENING

A family reunion event, which could be held in a half-term following MISSION:RESCUE, allows children to revisit the ideas and themes of the club and to show their families the kinds of thing they were involved in. Try to have as many of the MISSION:RESCUE team available as possible, as this will help children maintain the relationships they had at the club. Here is a suggested programme:

AGENTS' BRIEFING

As the children arrive, they should go to their Spy Rings to catch up with each other. Play a game where you throw a dice and then talk about a specific topic assigned to the number you throw. Topics could include 'What I remember about MISSION:RESCUE', 'What I did for the rest of my holidays' or 'What I like best about school'.

Meanwhile parents could either join in with the groups or have a drink in a cafe area, where photographs and pieces of artwork from the week are displayed. Make this environment as warm and welcoming as possible and ensure that a number of team members are available to talk to parents and welcome them as they arrive.

ACTIVE AGENTS
Sing the MISSION:RESCUE song and do one of the special operations from the club. Explain the stories and themes of each day at the club. You could retell the most popular story from the week too.

GOING UNDERCOVER
Play some of the most popular games from MISSION: RESCUE; you could even encourage the parents to take part!

SONG AND PRAYER
Choose a favourite song from the week to sing together, and then end with a prayer. Thank the parents for sending their children to the club and provide information about other up-and-coming events to be held at church.

FOOD
Share a simple meal together.

MIDWEEK CLUBS
An ideal way to maintain contact with children is to hold a midweek club at your church or local primary school. Scripture Union publishes **eye level** resources, aimed at midweek clubs for primary age children, especially those with no church background. Awesome is an **eye level** club recommended as a follow-up to MISSION: RESCUE. God's rescue plan continued and was fulfilled in Jesus.

So Why God?, another **eye level** club, is suitable if you have children who are interested in knowing more about being a Christian. It takes questions children ask about following Jesus and helps them to come up with an answer. It also leads children in a sensitive way through the process of becoming a Christian. (See the inside front cover for details of Awesome and So Why God?)

EXTENDED SCHOOLS INITIATIVE
All schools are required to offer care for children before and after school as part of the Extended Schools Initiative. A weekly MISSION:RESCUE club could become a fantastic follow-up to the holiday club, engaging with the children where they are already

at – in school. In negotiation with the head teacher and key members of staff, the club would be able to provide creative art workshops for children, including the telling of a Bible story and some opportunity for discussion. This will work best in small groups of no more than twelve children.

MISSION: RESCUE DAYS
Day events held throughout the year are good to maintain contact with holiday club children. These are effective when they coincide with a special time of the year: harvest, alternative Halloween, Christmas, new year, Valentine's Day, Easter. Here is a suggested programme:

REGISTRATION AND SPY RING GAMES
- **Active agents** (with story, teaching, songs, games etc)
- **Games**
- **Break**
- **Small-group Bible exploration**
- **Lunch**
- **Craft**
- **Break**
- **Agents are go!** (songs, Learn and remember verse, recap on story, Interrogation)
- **Agents debrief** time for interactive prayer and response time

It might also be possible to run additional MISSION: RESCUE days when the local school has an inset day. Gathering a team may be more difficult as many will be at work, but it can be of real service to the community and parents who will need to be at work themselves.

You can also adapt Awesome for use as various day programmes throughout the year. See the end of Awesome for more details.

FAMILY DAYS
The programme above need not be limited to children. There is something spiritual about families sharing and learning together. Ability is not necessary, and the children will enjoy helping other adults in activities with which they are comfortable. Therefore, one option is to hold a MISSION:RESCUE day where you invite the family members of the children who attended the holiday club (parents, siblings, grandparents, aunts/uncles, godparents are all welcome.)

X:SITE

X:site is a children's event for 7- to 11-year-olds. Each event takes place every two months in towns, cities or whole areas and combines silly games, live music, videos, creative prayer, craft, drama, Bible stories and lots more so that everyone can learn about Jesus and have fun at the same time!

X:site is a great way to encourage children in your church by bringing them together with other children in their community – they will have such a good time that they will want to invite their friends to come too. **X:site** is organised in each area by a partnership of local churches; Scripture Union is really keen to see more **X:site** events happening around the country. With your help there could be one nearer you.

Check out our website and if you want to get involved get in touch with us. We would really love to hear from you!

£5 OFF!

Buy £60 worth of extra **MISSION:RESCUE** resources and get £5 off!

Complete the name and address, tick the right boxes and cut out the voucher. Then:

- Take it to your local Christian bookshop.
- Send it to:
  Scripture Union Mail Order,
  PO Box 5148,
  Milton Keynes MLO,
  MK2 2YX
  with your order and payment.
- Visit our online shop at **www.scriptureunion.org.uk** and place your order online, where the £5 discount will be applied.

TITLE

NAME

ADDRESS

POSTCODE

EMAIL

We would like to keep in touch with you by placing you on our mailing list. Would you prefer to be contacted by:

☐ post

☐ email

☐ If you prefer not to be contacted, then please tick this box

Scripture Union does not sell or lease its lists.

ULTIMATE SERIES

Do you work with children or young people? Need that extra bit of inspiration to help your group explore the Bible? Want that extra idea to complete your session?

Then the ULTIMATE series is for you!

Each ULTIMATE book is packed full of ideas that have been used successfully by others and are more than likely to work for you! All at £9.99.

Ultimate Craft 978 1 84427 364 5
Ultimate Creative prayer 978 1 84427 367 6
Ultimate Games 978 1 84427365 2
Ultimate Quizzes 978 1 84427 366 9
Ultimate Visual Aids CD ROM 978 1 84427 355 3

Order from SU Mail Order
T 0845 07 06 006 **F** 01908 856 020
www.scriptureunion.org.uk/shop

This voucher cannot be exchanged for cash or any other merchandise, and connot be used with any other offer. This offer includes the MISSION:RESCUE resource book, MISSION:RESCUE DVD and Secret Files (singles and packs). It does not include CPO merchandise. Only orders of £60 and above qualify for this offer.

To the retailer: Please accept this voucher as a discount payment.

Credit due: £5.00 less normal trade discount.

This voucher must be returned by
3 September 2011 to:
Marston Book Services Ltd
PO Box 269
Abingdon
Oxfordshire
OX14 4YN

NAME OF SHOP

STL ACCOUNT NO

Cash value 0.0001p   **VOMR11**